HOW TO MAKE A QUILT

Learn Basic Sewing Techniques for Creating Patchwork Quilts and Projects

Barbara Weiland Talbert

Storey Publishing

*The mission of Storey Publishing is to serve our customers by
publishing practical information that encourages
personal independence in harmony with the environment.*

Edited by Gwen Steege and Kathy Brock
Series design by Alethea Morrison
Text production by Theresa Wiscovitch
Indexed by Eileen Clawson

Cover illustration by © Caitlin Keegan
Interior illustrations by Missy Shepler

Storey Publishing
210 MASS MoCA Way
North Adams, MA 01247
www.storey.com

Printed in the United States by McNaughton & Gunn, Inc.
10 9 8 7 6 5 4 3 2 1

LIBRARY OF CONGRESS CATALOGING-IN-PUBLICATION DATA

Talbert, Barbara Weiland, 1947–
  How to make a quilt / by Barbara Weiland Talbert.
     pages cm — (Storey basics)
  Includes index.
  ISBN 978-1-61212-408-7 (pbk. : alk. paper)
  ISBN 978-1-61212-409-4 (ebook) 1. Quilting. I. Title.
TT835.T275 2015
746.46—dc23
                                    2014020888

In memory of Marilyn Morse, my Morningstar,
who helped me find my authentic voice,
and for
Sheryl Reeder and Barbara Christenson,
my sisters of choice,
who always listen with their hearts.

CONTENTS

LET'S MAKE A QUILT

Making a quilt has become the quintessential American pastime. Although in vogue during many different eras in our history, quiltmaking began its meteoric rise in more recent popularity during the 1976 American Bicentennial. Now it's a beloved activity worldwide. Quilts appeal to our visual and tactile senses and to our need to create. If you love to sew and you love color and fabric, quiltmaking is tailor-made for you! And with new fabrics, new tools, and new techniques, it's easier than ever.

If you have basic sewing skills and you've yearned to make a quilt, or you need a refresher course on basic quiltmaking, you'll find what you need in this little handbook. If you haven't sewn in a while, you may want to take a brush-up course in basic sewing techniques at your favorite fabric store or sewing machine dealership, or ask a more experienced sewer to help you. Why not enlist a sewing buddy to learn how to make a quilt with you — it can be more fun when you share learning experiences and celebrate successes!

With a sewing machine, a few basic tools, and an assortment of colorful cotton fabrics, you're ready to get started. Before you know it, you will be making accurately stitched patchwork blocks to turn into pot holders, tote bags, small wall hangings, table toppers, and even larger lap- and bed-size quilts. You can practice the techniques shown in this book by making the blocks illustrated and then combine them into a quilt or use them to make several smaller projects. Make the nine sampler blocks illustrated in chapter 3 and you'll have enough to complete a quilted table topper or small wall hanging (see The Beginner's Sampler Quilt, page 114).

Note that this book features lessons in making patchwork blocks with geometric pieces, which require straight seaming. Blocks with curved pieces or triangles with sharp points are not included, as these require learning to make and use templates, slightly more advanced techniques. Appliqué, a method of adding figurative pieces to the surface of the blocks and borders, is also reserved for another book.

When you know how to cut and sew together a few basic patchwork shapes and turn them into a quilt, you will have the confidence you need to expand your skills and make hundreds of other block styles for your quilting projects. In addition to basic block cutting and assembly, you'll learn how to layer your finished quilt top with batting and backing, machine-quilt them together, and finally finish your project with binding and a label.

WHAT MAKES A QUILT A QUILT?

A TRADITIONAL PIECED QUILT has three essential layers:

- **Blocks,** which may be joined with plain squares or other shapes to make the quilt-top center
- **Filler,** usually batting, or sometimes flannel or other fabric
- **Backing,** to cover the batting on the back of the quilt

In addition, you usually find the following on quilts:

- **Quilting stitches** to hold the layers together
- **Binding** to finish the edges
- **Outer border** (most quilts have at least one) and sometimes **sashing strips** and **cornerstones** that connect the block rows.

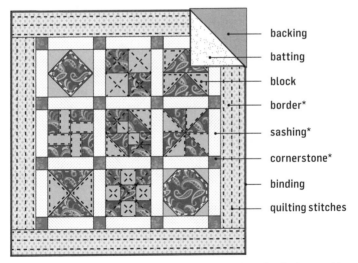

- backing
- batting
- block
- border*
- sashing*
- cornerstone*
- binding
- quilting stitches

*Most quilts have borders; some have multiple borders. Not all quilts have sashing and cornerstones.

CHAPTER 1

GET READY

You don't need a fancy machine to make a quilt, just one that is in good working order with well-adjusted tension. And you don't need a lot of new sewing skills. In fact, if you have made home-dec items or clothing, you probably already have most of the sewing skills you need! However, you may need to purchase some additional cutting and sewing tools that are specially designed to enhance and assist the quiltmaking experience.

If you can cut straight and stitch a straight, accurate ¼"-wide seam allowance, you can make quilt blocks and sew them together to make a quilt top. Even your first machine-quilting stitches can be lines of straight stitching. You can graduate to more complex quilting designs after you are comfortable with basic machine quilting.

GATHERING TOOLS AND SUPPLIES: THE QUILTER'S TOOLBOX

LIKE ANY HOBBY, quiltmaking requires special materials and tools designed for specific tasks. In times past, quilt pieces were cut with scissors from fabric leftovers, feed sacks, and worn clothing. Today's quiltmakers can choose from a dizzying array of quality quilters' cottons. While patches were once sewn together and the quilting done by hand, today's modern tools and techniques make it easy to cut multiple pieces quickly and sew them together by machine. Piecing and quilting the layers together by machine is now more popular than piecing and quilting by hand because it takes less time and you can see the results sooner! That's what's covered in this book.

As a sewer, you may already have most, if not all, of the tools you need. There are lots of new, innovative quiltmaking tools available, but you can make many quilt blocks using a few basic tools and techniques. Here's what you need to get started. Some will be shown in illustrations in the following chapters.

Sewing Machine and Accessories

- **A well-maintained sewing machine** makes piecing quicker and easier than sewing by hand.
- **A ¼" quilters' presser foot** assists in stitching accurate piecing seams.
- **A walking foot or even-feed feature** on your machine prevents layers from shifting when machine quilting and sewing on the binding.

- **Size 75/11 or 80/12 sharp needles.** Topstitch and Microtex needles are sharps; universal needles will work for your first projects, but sharps stitch through quilters' cottons more easily for a finer seam and accurate, straight stitches. Special quilter's machine needles with specially tapered points for accurate piecing are also available.

Cutting Tools

- **An 18" × 24" rotary cutting mat with self-healing surface** is essential. It should have a printed grid of 1" squares to help with fabric and ruler alignment. (You may want to invest in a larger one later.)

For Safety's Sake

- *Remember that rotary cutters are razor sharp!*

- *Always roll the cutter away from you on the mat when cutting.*

- *Always engage the cutter's safety guard before you put it down.*

- *Keep the cutter out of the reach of children and pets.*

- *After removing dull blades, tape them inside a piece of cardboard before disposing.*

- **Standard or large heavy-duty rotary cutter.** Today's cutters have many options: handle shape and design, color, quick-release blade changing, and self-retracting blades. Test several to determine what is most comfortable for your hand. (*Note:* Rotary cutting tools appear on pages 27–30.)
- **Acrylic rotary rulers** provide an edge to cut along for accurate pieces. They are $1/8$" thick and come in an array of lengths and widths. They are marked in $1/8$" increments with many horizontal and vertical lines. Some have angled lines for help when cutting diamonds and sharp-pointed triangles. For your first one, invest in a 6" × 24" acrylic ruler. This is a standard size that is essential for cutting strips; every quilter should have one. It's also good to have a 4" × 12" ruler for cutting smaller pieces from the strips and a 6"-square rotary ruler to use when cutting small pieces.

Hand-Sewing Tools

- **Small sewing or embroidery scissors** for clipping threads and trimming seams.
- **Sharp hand-sewing needles,** size 11 or 12 for general sewing, and in assorted sizes for attaching binding by hand. Shorter needles make finer stitches; the higher the number, the shorter and finer the needle.
- **Thimble** that fits without being too tight, to protect your finger while you hand-sew binding and a label to your finished project.
- Sharp **seam ripper** for undoing or removing inaccurate stitching.

Miscellaneous Tools and Supplies

- **Ironing board (or surface) and an iron** with steam setting (you will use dry and steam settings). Look for an iron with a smooth soleplate and enough weight to make a difference when pressing.
- **Masking tape** for securing layers when preparing the "quilt sandwich" (page 86)
- **1¾"-long quilter's pins** or flower-head pins and a pincushion or magnetic pin dish.
- **Curved, rustproof safety pins**, size 1 or 1½, for holding quilt layers together for machine quilting.
- **Oval quilt clips** to keep quilts rolled and out of the way of the needle when quilting the layers together.
- **Temporary spray adhesive** for holding quilt layers together in lieu of pins.
- **Water-soluble or air-soluble marking pen and a fine-lead pencil** for marking matching points and quilting lines.
- **Chalk wheel with powdered chalk** for marking quilting lines.

PREPARING YOUR SEWING MACHINE

MAKE SEWING A BREEZE by preparing your machine for optimal stitching.

- Make sure your machine is in good working order and remove any lint in the bobbin area — it can interfere with smooth stitching.
- Wind two bobbins before you start a quilting project so you'll be able to quickly resume stitching when the first one runs out.
- Thread the machine correctly and insert the bobbin. Draw the bobbin thread to the top so both thread tails are easy to grasp.
- Set the stitch length to 2.5 mm (12 stitches per inch).
- For block assembly, insert a new needle. Size 75/11 or 80/12 sharps (Microtex and topstitching needles) are recommended (page 6). Replace your needle after 8 to 10 hours of sewing. A dull needle will snag even cotton fabrics and can create inaccurate seaming.
- Test the tension and balance it so stitches interlock between the two layers of the cotton fabric in your project, and are not lying loosely on the top or bottom layer of fabric. Check your machine manual for instructions.

CHOOSING A QUILT PROJECT

IF YOU ARE NEW TO QUILTING, choose a small project, labeled as a "beginner" or "easy" design. A small quilt with a few blocks, plus sashing and a border, can be an easy way to start. Use it as a table topper or wall hanging. You can make practice blocks from this book (see chapter 3) and quickly turn them into quilted pot holders or placemats. Or make them and sew them together into the featured nine-block sampler quilt (page 114).

Look for designs that have blocks no smaller than 6" square. Larger 9", 10", or 12" blocks with bigger patches are super easy and fast to piece, but smaller blocks are often more visually interesting. Squares, rectangles, and right-angle triangles are the easiest pieces to cut and sew together. Steer clear of blocks with curved seams and those with sharp-pointed triangles until you have some block-piecing skills under your belt.

Once you've learned the basics while making practice blocks, you'll be ready to choose other blocks and quilt designs from the myriad quilt books available for beginners, or from individual quilt patterns offered at quilt shops and online sources.

SELECTING FABRIC

FOR ANY PROJECT, YOU WILL NEED fabric to make the blocks for your quilted project, as well as fabrics for the borders, backing, and edge binding. You'll also need batting for the inner layer. Quilts can be made from a wide array of fabrics, but for beginners, the best fabric is good quality 100% cotton fabric especially designed for quiltmaking. Find quality quilters' cottons at your local quilt shop, and don't be afraid to ask for help when choosing fabrics for your project. Quilt shop personnel — and other shoppers, too — are usually very willing to assist with pattern and fabric selection when you need help.

Quilters' cottons are specially made with a higher thread count (the number of threads per inch) to minimize raveling. They may also be more colorfast than fabrics designed for other purposes. Don't use low-quality fabric with low thread count or a loose weave. Low-quality fabrics are more difficult to handle, and, since you will be cutting many pieces and sewing them together, the raveling associated with low-thread-count cottons can affect accuracy in the finished blocks.

It may be tempting to use less expensive fabrics when you are a beginning quilter, but I advise against it. Lower quality cottons often lose body after washing, and they wrinkle more, making accurate piecing more difficult. Your efforts deserve better fabric for the best possible experience. To save on fabrics for your first blocks, check out a shop's sales area, where you'll find lower prices on bolts that are running low or are out of season. Watch for seasonal sales, too. My cardinal rule for buying fabric: Buy fabric you love in the best quality you can afford — you'll be glad you did.

Choosing fabric is one of the most fun and enjoyable parts of quiltmaking. As a beginner, you may want to rely on the pattern you are using for fabric cues. If you're a skilled seamstress with a well-developed sense of color, pattern, scale, and design coordination, fabric choice will come more easily. Beginners may find it easy to simply copy the color scheme shown in the pattern they are following — but not necessarily with the same fabrics. By the time most books and patterns are in print, the specific fabric prints and colors shown are often no longer available or are difficult to find. If you love the design but not the color scheme in the pattern, substitute fabrics in a color palette you love.

A majority of the block designs you will use in patchwork quilts are made of two or more fabrics in two or more colors. The success of your project will depend on how well you select fabrics for the right amount of contrast in the patches within the blocks. When there is good contrast in value (lightness compared to darkness), the desired design in each block and in the completed project is easy to see.

Color in quilts is a subject large enough to explore in long chapters and in full-length books; two good ones are named in the Reading List on page 119. Following are some basic guidelines for choosing fabric for your quilts.

Color and Value Basics

It's easy to select fabrics for a two-color quilt: Choose one light background print and one medium or dark print. Red and white, blue and white, tan and black, pink and ecru — there's an endless list of possible two-color combinations. If you opt for this scheme, you may use only two fabrics, one light print and one dark, or you may choose several fabrics that are in the same color family of each of the two colors for more variation and visual interest. Choosing several fabrics is a "scrappier" approach, and many quilters love scrap quilts.

DIFFERENT VALUES create contrast.

CHANGING VALUE POSITIONS in the same block design creates a different look.

When the design requires several different colors, you must pay attention to the color value of the fabrics. *Value* is the relative lightness or darkness when fabrics are placed next to each other. (Refer to the illustrations on the previous page.) Most patterns tell you what values you need with these descriptors: very light, light, medium light, medium, medium dark, dark, and very dark. However, as you select your own fabrics, you will need to determine if each of them stands out as a dark, shows up as a mid value, or "sits back" in the finished block as a light value. Also note on the previous page how two blocks of the same design can look very different, depending on where the values are placed.

A Trick for Determining Value

1. *Purchase a transparent red plastic-sheet binder and cut it in half along the fold. Take one piece with you to the quilt shop.*

2. *Stack or fan your fabric choices on the cutting counter.*

3. *Stand back and hold the red sheet in front of the fabrics. In most fabrics, you will be able to clearly see the darkness or lightness of the fabrics in relationship to each other. Unfortunately, this doesn't work with predominantly red fabrics; you'll have to squint instead.*

When you use fabrics in a block that are very close to each other in values, the colors tend to "moosh" together, creating a softer and less obvious design in the blocks and the project overall.

When shopping for fabric, an easy way to determine relative value is to stack the bolts of fabric you've chosen, or fan them out on the cutting counter, and step back. Through squinted eyes, look for fabrics in the stack that seem to blend into each other too much; if necessary, substitute new fabric(s) for one or more of them to create more contrast in the values. This takes a little practice; get help from the quilt shop's sales staff.

Combining Prints in Quiltmaking

Pay attention to the scale of the printed design in each fabric you've chosen. Varying print types and motif scales makes designs more interesting. Too many large prints will probably moosh together, and lots of tiny prints will do the same thing. Better to combine fabrics with a range of motif sizes and types so they will stand out from each other.

Strategies for Selecting Fabric

Don't let fabric selection stop you in your tracks. Instead, use one or more of these strategies to develop your confidence:

- Study the pattern you are following for color values and print scale. Try to select similar-looking fabrics in your desired color palette.

- Begin with a multicolor focus print (see Fabric Selection Checklist, page 17) of medium- or large-scale motifs — a large floral, for example. Look for a dark- or medium-value print with at least three colors that you love. Use it as your inspiration to select other fabrics that will work with it. Use the squint test to see what they will look like when used together in the blocks. You aren't obligated to use this focus fabric in your actual project — it can just be a guide in color selection. Of course, go ahead and use it if you love it with the other fabrics you select.

....

Pre-Cuts: Fat Quarters, Fat Eighths, and Others

When you need only ¼ yard of fabric, some patterns call for *fat quarters*, which measure 18" × 22" (the equivalent in square inches of a ¼ yard of 44"/45"-wide fabric). They are perfect when you need a small amount of a fabric and for building up a selection of colors and prints that you like for future projects. (This fabric collection is fondly referred to as a *quilter's stash*.) Most quilt shops offer fat-quarter bundles in a wide array of prints and colors as well as by the single piece. *Fat eighths* (9" × 22") may also be available.

Manufacturers now offer other packets of pre-cuts as well. Charm packs of 5" pre-cut squares are popular, as well as 10"-square *layer cakes* and rolls of 2½"-wide strips (*jelly rolls*). These squares and strip rolls offer a variety of fabrics that are already color-coordinated and cut into commonly used sizes. Look for patterns designed specifically for these fabric groupings. Of course you can cut smaller pieces from any of the pre-cuts.

....

- If a pattern calls for a solid color(s), substitute a mottled tone-on-tone print (also called a "low-volume" print) or a tiny print that reads as a solid from a distance or when using the squint test. These prints are a quilter's best friend because they help hide inaccuracies in piecing and quilting that stand out more clearly in a solid fabric. Subtle variations in color, value, and shading in tone-on-tone prints add movement and visual interest that you won't get with solids. Of course, that's not to say you cannot or should not use solid fabrics — some designs require solids for the desired effect. Traditional Amish-style quilts are a good example.
- Check out the fat-quarter bundles and other pre-cut fabric groupings (see the sidebar on the facing page) offered by many quilt shops. These are often perfectly color-and-value-coordinated fabric groupings from a single manufacturer's line that work well together. You may need to supplement these pre-cuts with additional fabrics.
- If all else fails, ask for help! Another pair of eyes is always a good test!

Fabric Selection Checklist

After choosing fabrics, use the list on the next page as a guide to make sure the combination you've chosen includes the suggested types listed, which will result in a pleasing overall design. If you are in doubt about how a fabric will work, it's a good idea to buy a little more fabric than required. This provides the leeway to make test blocks as the final check of your selections and replace one or more fabrics if necessary. Add unused fabrics to your stash.

- **Focus print or theme fabric.** This should exhibit a range of colors that fits into the color scheme you've chosen.
- **Contrast.** Look for varying values in relationship to each other (lights, mediums, and darks) for depth and definition in the quilt blocks.
- **Visual variety.** Include varying print scales for interest and to move the eye across and around the quilt. This prevents prints and colors from disappearing into each other in the quilt top.
- **Zing.** Throw in an accent color — a small amount of a bright, richly saturated color or one that is unexpected. A little goes a long way, and you probably won't want one at all in softer, more muted color schemes.

Border, Backing, and Binding Fabrics

It's best to choose border, backing, and binding fabrics when you select the fabrics for your quilt top. You are more likely to find fabrics that work with the block fabrics then, rather than waiting until you've finished the blocks — which could be a while depending on your available time. Fabric manufacturers develop new color palettes and print designs frequently, which means last year's pink is usually not the same as this year's.

Choose quilters' cottons for the borders, backing, and binding so they will handle and launder the same as the fabrics in your blocks. For the backing, choose a print with colors that complement the colors on the front of your quilt. A busy print for the backing is a great choice because it will help hide stitching imperfections in the quilting stitches.

For small projects that finish to less than 36" square, a 40" square of fabric will work (purchase 1⅛ or 1¼ yards of 44"/45" fabric for this). For projects that finish larger, you will need to make a pieced backing as discussed on page 89. Some shops carry wider quilters' cottons for backing, but the prints and colors are limited.

For the binding fabric, choose the same fabric as your border if you want the binding to "disappear." A contrasting binding will act like a narrow frame around the quilt.

Preparing Your Fabric

Quilters' cottons are usually 44" or 45" wide, sold by the yard or in smaller pre-cut pieces. Some may be as narrow as 40". The fabrics have two *selvages* — tightly woven edges along the lengthwise grain. Most cotton fabrics shrink 1 to 3 percent during laundering. Although some quiltmakers never prewash their fabrics, I recommend preshrinking cotton fabrics if you plan to launder the finished quilt. It's best to have shrinkage occur *before* you assemble your project, unless shrinkage doesn't matter to you. Preshrinking also helps eliminate excess dye to ensure colorfastness in your finished project.

After laundering, your fabric will not be as long and possibly not as wide as the original cut. Most quilt-pattern designers give generous yardage requirements in their patterns so you will have enough fabric for your project after shrinkage.

HOW TO PRESHRINK FABRIC

1. To preshrink, wash similar colors in a mild detergent and hot water. This will remove any excess chemicals and dyes from the fabric that may remain after manufacturing. If you are concerned about color loss and bleeding, use Retayne, a dye fixative, in the wash as directed by the manufacturer. For small cuts of fabric, including fat quarters and fat eighths, I suggest machine-basting the two raw edges together ½" from the edge so the piece doesn't twist or knot up in the washing machine. Remove the basting before you iron the fabric. I also often launder small cuts of fabric zipped into mesh laundry bags.

2. Tumble-dry fabrics until barely damp to make ironing easier.

3. Set a dry iron on the cotton setting to press and remove wrinkles. Use steam or dampen as needed if your fabrics are dry and/or have deep wrinkles.

4. Apply spray starch to add back the body that was lost in the wash. Returning the fabric to a crisper hand will make it easier to handle, help with cutting accuracy, and deter raveling at cut edges.

SELECTING AND PREPARING BATTING

IN MOST QUILTS, a layer of fibers called *batting* is used between the quilt-top and backing layers for added loft and warmth. Batting *loft* (or thickness) also adds surface dimension when you quilt the layers together. Batting is made of a wide range of fibers and blends, including cotton, silk, wool, bamboo, and polyester. For the beginner, I recommend a low-loft, lightweight cotton or cotton-blend batting because it will be easier to handle and quilt, especially when quilting by machine. You can experiment with other types and thicknesses as you develop more skill and preferences and learn more from teachers and fellow quiltmakers.

For best results, remove batting from the packaging and open it out to relax for a day or two before you layer and quilt your project. If necessary, steam out any wrinkles, paying attention to fiber content and the recommended iron temperature. Air-fluff polyester batting in your dryer to remove deep wrinkles. Take care not to stretch the batting. Also read the manufacturer's guidelines for the best spacing distance for the quilting stitches in order to keep the batting in place inside your quilt. You'll need that information later.

CHOOSING THREAD

USING THE BEST THREAD for piecing is also important for success. Don't settle for a bargain-basement thread that will shred, kink, knot, break, and shed too much lint. Thread is what holds your quilt together — it's not a place to skimp on quality just to save a few pennies.

To piece your blocks, choose a color that closely matches or blends with your fabric colors, or use a neutral color — tan or gray — to blend with all the colors. The goal is to not see the thread color on the right side along the seamlines.

Use 60-weight high-quality polyester or cotton/poly-blend thread for piecing the blocks. All-purpose sewing thread is good, but some quilters use an even finer thread for piecing blocks for better seam accuracy. Thicker thread takes up more room in the seamline and affects final measurements of pieced blocks. The higher the number size on the spool, the finer the thread: a 60-weight thread is finer than 50-weight.

CHAPTER 2

ESSENTIAL SKILLS
CUTTING, SEWING, AND PRESSING

The most traditional pieced quilts are made of square blocks composed of a number of patches of fabric: a "patchwork" quilt. The patches are cut and then sewn together following a block layout. Piecing accurate blocks that fit together relies on mastering three essential skills: accurate cutting, precise sewing, and careful pressing. Slight errors in any step of block assembly add up to bigger ones, resulting in patches that won't fit together right and/or blocks that are not the right size or shape.

The focus of this book is on making easy blocks with pieces you can rotary-cut from fabric strips and squares. This requires cutting strips and patches of the correct size (which is stated in the block pattern you choose to follow). The strip and patch sizes include ¼"-wide seam allowances all around. This seam-allowance width is different from the standard ⅝"-seam width for garments, and the ½" standard for home dec items. You will also use a ¼"-wide seam allowance to join the completed blocks to make the quilt-top center and add the borders.

Mastering accurate cutting and sewing before pressing are both essential for a successful quilting project. And pressing patchwork requires special attention, too.

ROTARY CUTTING BASICS

OLD-TIME QUILTMAKERS USED templates to mark their patches and scissors to cut them, but you won't use either. Today's rotary cutter and mat, along with an acrylic ruler, make it possible to quickly cut squares, rectangles, and triangles — the most basic patch shapes in many block designs. Cutting each of these shapes begins with cutting strips from the appropriate fabric for the block design you are following. From the strips, you will crosscut the required squares and rectangles. If you need triangles, you will cut squares and then rotary-cut those into triangles.

To begin, prepare the fabric for cutting as directed beginning on page 19. Then gather your rotary-cutting tools and place the cutting mat, grid side up, on your cutting table; a kitchen counter is a good alternative cutting space.

Cutting Strips

Refer to your quilt pattern for the width and number of strips to cut across the width of each fabric. Strips will be approximately 40" to 44" long, depending on how much the fabric shrinks if you wash it before you begin cutting (page 20). Don't be surprised that different fabrics are different widths after pre-shrinking, even if they were all labeled 44"/45" wide. If using fat quarters or eighths (page 16), the strips will usually be between 20" and 22" long. (Take care to cut strips parallel to the longest edge of these pre-cuts, unless the directions specify otherwise.)

There are two rules you should remember when cutting strips.

- **Strip Width Rule #1:** For squares and rectangles, cut all strips ½" wider than the desired finished width in the block. This allows for the standard ¼"-wide seam allowance at each edge.
- **Strip Width Rule #2:** For squares that will be cut into triangles, cut strips and squares that are more than ½" wider than the finished patch size in the finished block. That's because you need enough seam allowance on the diagonal edges for joining them to other pieces in the blocks. Just follow the pattern for the correct strip width.

HOW TO CUT STRIPS

1. Iron the fabric to remove creases and wrinkles if necessary. Fold it in half lengthwise with selvages aligned, and smooth the layers together so there are no wrinkles along the folded edge. Don't worry about aligning the short raw edges if they don't match up. You will do a clean-up cut to straighten the cut edges *before* cutting strips from each fabric; this is different from garment and home-dec sewing, where accurate grainline is essential for things to hang correctly.

2. Fold the fabric in half lengthwise again, with the folded edge smooth, flat, and wrinkle-free. Align the just-folded edge along a grid line close to you on the cutting mat.

3. To make the clean-up cut, place the 6" × 24" acrylic ruler on top, just inside the cut edges, and align one of the horizontal inch-lines with the folded edge. Release the blade on the cutter, and then position your other hand firmly on the ruler with fingers spread to secure the ruler width so it won't slip. Use firm and steady pressure as you press the blade into the fabric layers and roll *away from you* right along the ruler edge to the selvages. Cut as far as is comfortable, then carefully lift and replace your hand on the ruler to continue cutting across the fabric width. With practice, you will be able to "walk" your fingers up the ruler. Discard the cutaway strip.

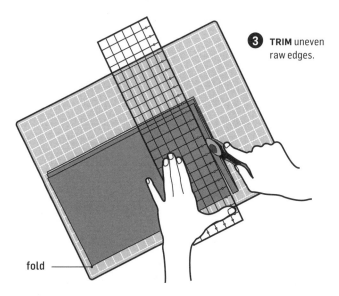

3 **TRIM** uneven raw edges.

fold

4. If you can walk around your cutting table to the opposite side, do so. If not, carefully lift and turn the just-cut edges and reposition the fabric on your cutting mat with the folded edge along one line and the cut edges along a perpendicular line. When everything is perfectly aligned, you're ready to cut strips.

5. Place the ruler on the fabric with a horizontal line perfectly aligned with the fabric's folded edge. Position the line for the desired strip width along the clean-cut edges. If the horizontal ruler line is not perfectly aligned with the fold, adjust and check the ruler alignment with the cut edge again. With the ruler perfectly positioned, cut along the ruler as described for the clean-up cut in step 3 (see the illustration on the next page).

(continued on next page)

6. After cutting the first strip, open it to make sure it is straight along both cut edges without a bend in it, or what I call a "wonky" strip. If the strip is not straight, set it aside, refold the fabric, do a new clean-up cut at the raw edges so they are straight, and then cut another strip. It's a good idea to stop and check the cut edges of the folded fabric after cutting every set of two or three strips, and then do another clean-up cut if necessary before cutting more strips. Remember, slight errors in cutting will add up to big ones when the patches are sewn together.

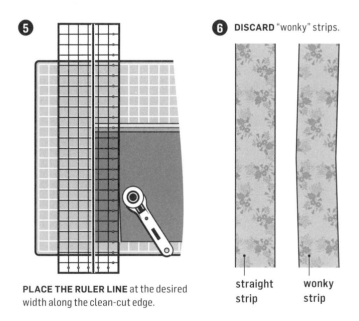

5

PLACE THE RULER LINE at the desired width along the clean-cut edge.

6 **DISCARD** "wonky" strips.

straight strip   wonky strip

Cutting Squares, Rectangles, and Triangles

Simple shapes, such as squares, rectangles, and triangles, are used in many traditional block patterns. Check your pattern for the required strip width to cut for each of these patch shapes in the block. Work with one fabric at a time and cut the required strips before cutting the patches from them.

HOW TO CUT SIMPLE SHAPES

1. After cutting the strips as directed in your quilt pattern, use a small square rotary ruler to cut away the selvages on each cut strip. They are too stiff to include in your patches. Make sure the cut is perpendicular to the long cut edges.

2. Fold each strip in half crosswise to make four layers. The folded edge must be smooth and flat, with all raw edges perfectly aligned before you cut.

3. **For squares and rectangles:** Position the ruler across the strip with the line for the desired width of the patchwork square or rectangle aligned with the short cut edges. Cut across the layers. Continue in this fashion until you have cut the required number of pieces for your project.

PLACE THE RULER line at the desired square size aligned with cut edges.

(continued on next page)

- **For half-square triangles:** First cut strips and then squares of the required size. Cut the squares in half diagonally from corner to corner. The diagonal edge is on the bias in each triangle; take care not to stretch it.

- **For quarter-square triangles,** first cut strips and then squares of the required size; next cut half-square triangles as described above. *Without moving the just-cut triangles,* reposition the ruler diagonally across them so you can cut them in half diagonally in the opposite direction. The two shorter adjacent edges of the triangles are on the bias; the longer edge is on the straight of grain.

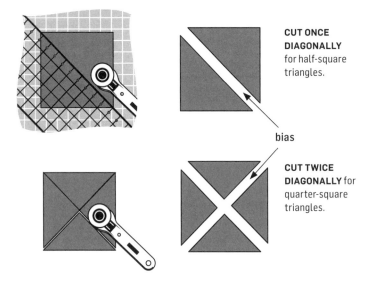

CUT ONCE DIAGONALLY for half-square triangles.

bias

CUT TWICE DIAGONALLY for quarter-square triangles.

There are many other geometric shapes that can be cut from strips. When you need a special shape, the pattern will give you a method for cutting it, using one of many specialty rulers or ready-made acrylic templates available in a range of sizes for block patches. Alternatively, you may be directed to use one of the angled lines on a standard rotary ruler to cut the shapes. To learn more about making and using patchwork templates, check out *The Quilting Answer Book* (see Resources and Links on page 118) or other basic guides to cutting patchwork shapes.

There are also easy ways to rotary-cut some blocks that would normally require templates. For example, the classic Snowball block (page 64) requires an octagon and four half-square triangles. However, you can avoid using a template for the center octagon, and then cutting and sewing triangles to the angled edges, by substituting the folded-corner piecing method (page 56). With this method, you will cut only squares to make the classic Snowball block.

Strip Width Rule #3

There is a third rule to remember when cutting strips: Measure twice, cut once to avoid errors. Every time you get ready to make the next cut, take the time to position the ruler and then double-check it before cutting. Be especially careful when measurements are in ⅛" increments, as in 3⅞".

STITCHING A PERFECT SEAM

Before you start sewing, take the time to make sure you can stitch the standard-width patchwork seam. This is critical so that all the patches in the blocks will fit together perfectly — and so that all the blocks will fit together to assemble the quilt top.

There may be a ¼"-seam guideline engraved on the bed of your machine, but maybe not. Even if there is, don't trust it until you've tested it as detailed below. Many modern quilters now rely on a ¼" presser foot, also called a *patchwork foot*, designed specifically for quiltmaking. You can probably purchase one for your machine if it wasn't provided. It's worth the investment! This foot is designed so that the distance from the center needle position to either outer edge of the foot is a scant ¼".

Why a scant seam allowance? Unlike traditional sewing, both seam allowances in patchwork blocks are usually pressed to one side rather than open. This results in a slight loss of width in the finished unit because of the "turn of cloth" when the seam allowances are both pressed in the same direction. Sewing a seam that is a thread or two narrower than ¼" makes up for this loss. The ¼" foot for your machine may also have handy marks along the outer edges to help you stop exactly where you need to when applying the binding to the finished quilt.

Whether you use a guide on the machine or a ¼" foot, you must test the seam width and adjust your stitching if necessary to perfect your seaming technique. Even if the difference in your seam width is only ¹⁄₁₆" wider than ¼", that adds up to ½" if your block has three patches across and three patches down, as in a Ninepatch block (page 59); in this case, a block that should finish to 9" square would end up only 8½" square. The reverse is also true: if the seam is too narrow, the finished block will be larger than required. Either way, the difference will really affect the finished size of your project if there are lots of seams and lots of blocks!

HOW TO SEW ¼" SEAM ALLOWANCES

1. On a piece of ¼" graph paper, with four squares to the inch, make sure the first row at the right-hand edge has no margin and is ¼" wide. If it isn't, trim as needed.

2. Place the graph paper on the bed of your machine and adjust the position so you can lower the needle into the paper, just *barely to the right of the first line* at the right-hand edge of the paper (page 34). Make sure the paper is straight and parallel to any stitching guidelines on the machine bed and lower the presser foot to hold it in place.

3. Rotary-cut a ⅜"-wide strip of Dr. Scholl's moleskin (or other similar sticky-back foam product). It should be long enough to extend 2" in front of the presser foot toes and at least 1" behind the back edge of the presser foot. Remove the paper backing and adhere the foam strip to the machine right next to the edge of the paper. If the strip will interfere with the feed dogs, carefully cut a notch in the foam strip as shown on the next page so it will fit around them.

(continued on next page)

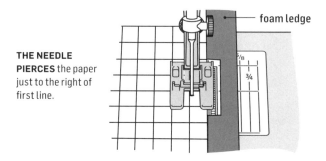

THE NEEDLE
PIERCES the paper
just to the right of
first line.

foam ledge

Note: Even if the foam strip actually aligns perfectly with the edge of your ¼" foot or with a line on the machine, it's a good idea to leave it in place. It creates a ledge against which to guide the fabric layers as you sew, making it easy to prevent the edges from wandering, for a perfect seam allowance every time! That means no guesswork for a beginner — and even for old pros! If using pins, though, you will need to pin with the points toward the raw edge; otherwise the pin heads will run into the ledge.

There's one more option for accurate ¼" seams. If you don't have a ¼" foot, use the regular straight-stitch presser foot and adjust the seam width by moving the needle position so you can use the edge of the foot as a guide.

After you've established the perfect seam width following the guidelines on the facing page, you will be ready to cut and sew patches together for your blocks.

Before you start piecing blocks, always test the seam allowance on actual fabric patches.

HOW TO CHECK SEAM ALLOWANCES

1. Rotary-cut two 3" squares of fabric (page 29), making
    sure the cuts are accurate. Place right sides together with
    all raw edges aligned.

2. Place the patches under the presser foot and stitch with
    the right-hand raw edges against the foam ledge (if you
    are using it; see the previous how-to) or with the presser
    foot perfectly aligned with the right-hand raw edges.
    Watch the edge of the foot, *not* the needle, as you stitch.

    Don't backstitch at the beginning and end of a seam as
    you normally do with other types of sewing. Try to break
    that habit when making patchwork blocks; the backstitched
    area will have more thread in it than the remainder of the
    seam. This adversely affects seam accuracy because press-
    ing backstitched areas perfectly flat is more difficult.

    Some quiltmakers suggest adjusting the stitch length
    to 2.00 mm (15 stitches per inch) to ensure that the
    beginning and ending stitches won't come undone as you
    work with your blocks; however, this will make it a bit
    more difficult to "unstitch seams" if you make an error!
    For the safest way to remove incorrect stitching, see Seam
    Ripping: A Necessary Skill on the next page.

3. Press along the stitches to set the thread into the seam,
    and then flip to the right side. Use a dry iron to press
    both seam allowances toward one of the squares.

(continued on next page)

4. Check the width from edge to edge across the seam in the resulting two-patch unit; it should measure exactly 5½". If it doesn't, adjust the needle position one step to the right for a narrower seam or one step to the left for a slightly wider seam. Cut another set of patches and test again.

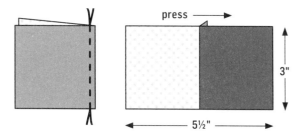

Seam Ripping: A Necessary Skill

No matter how careful you are, stitching mistakes are inevitable. When "unstitching" a seam or section of a seam is necessary, slip the tip of a sharp seam ripper or double-pointed scissors under every sixth stitch on the bobbin-thread side of the seamline. (For some reason, bobbin threads are easier to clip.) How do you know which is which? Use different color threads in the needle and the bobbin, for example, tan on top, gray on the bottom. After clipping from the bobbin side, it should be easy to pull on the top thread and lift it away from the seamline. Use a piece of masking tape to make it easy to remove the bobbin-thread tufts left behind on the wrong side. Be careful not to stretch any bias edges when removing stitching.

CUTTING AND STITCHING PRACTICE

The simplest of quilt tops is made of squares joined together in as many rows as desired. Depending on fabric choices, these simple quilts can be quite exciting and modern looking. Cutting and sewing together lots of squares provides lots of practice with sewing accurate seams and then assembling them into a quilt top following the directions provided in chapter 4, adding borders if you wish. Finish your quilt following the directions in chapter 5.

1. Begin by cutting 5"-wide strips from seven of your favorite fabrics, then crosscut 5" squares from the strips. You should get eight squares from a 40"-long strip. That makes 56 squares.

2. Arrange the squares as desired in eight rows of seven squares each.

3. Sew each row of squares together with the ¼"-wide seam allowance you've established.

4. Arrange the rows in the desired order and press the seam allowances in opposite directions from row to row, following the pressing guidelines in Press It Right on the next page. Set the pressed rows aside to use later when learning how to assemble a quilt top and add borders in chapter 4.

PRESS IT RIGHT

CAREFUL PRESSING IS ESSENTIAL for fitting blocks together perfectly. Heavy-handed ironing is *not* pressing and can distort your blocks; too much steam can cause unwanted shrinkage. Most quilt patterns direct you to press patchwork seam allowances to one side, not open, making it easier to match seam intersections when sewing block pieces together and when joining blocks into rows to complete the quilt top. This is often referred to as *pressing for opposing seams*. See the example in the illustration below. It's also generally agreed that pressing seam allowances to one side results in a stronger, more durable quilt top that will better withstand wear and repeated laundering.

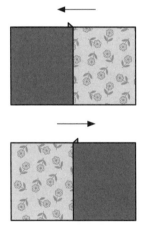

FOLLOW PRESSING ARROWS to press seams in opposing directions.

Do You Iron or Do You Press?

It's important to know the difference!

Iron your fabrics before cutting the pieces. Move the iron back and forth with downward pressure to remove all wrinkles and restore the fabric's shape. Use a steam iron if necessary, but be careful not to stretch the fabric out of shape or off-grain.

Press seam allowances to coax them into a specified position. Pressing is a simple up-and-down motion. Use your fingers to arrange the seam allowance in the desired direction. Lower the iron, press down, and then lift it to move to the next seam or section of a long seam. To avoid distorting the blocks and moving already-pressed allowances into undesired positions, do not push the iron along the seam allowances.

Patchwork Pressing Details

For best results when pressing seams in patchwork blocks and quilt tops, remember the following tips.

- **Press along all stitching lines to set the stitches and the thread for a flatter, crisper seamline.** Then press seam allowances in the desired direction. It's easiest to press from the right side, using the tip of the iron to press over the seam allowances lying underneath. Pressing seam allowances in this manner creates a tiny fabric "ledge" at the seamline — a high and low side of the seam. Since you can see the seamline on the right side of the block, it also results in flat seamlines, with no little tucks or pleats of fabric obscuring them.

- **Follow the pressing directions or arrows in your pattern.** The general rule for pressing patchwork seam allowances is to press *both* of them toward the darker patch in a unit, so the darker fabric won't shadow through the lighter one. However, this rule is broken on purpose all the time — to make it easier to join units in many patchwork blocks and to join pieced blocks to pieced blocks. If you must press seam allowances toward the lighter fabric, after stitching the seam trim the darker seam allowance just a bit narrower than the light one for less shadow-through on the block's right side.
- **Press seams in opposing directions on pieced units that will be joined.** This makes it easy to snugly "nest" the opposing high and low sides of the seamline into each other for perfect matching at seam intersections. It distributes seam allowance bulk evenly on each side of the joining seam. It also facilitates quilting-in-the-ditch (page 97).
- **Any seam that will be crossed by another must be pressed first.**

HOW TO PRESS PATCHWORK UNITS

1. Use the cotton setting for quilters' cottons and little or no steam to prevent unwanted block shrinkage and distortion. (It's easier to unknowingly stretch damp fabrics out of shape when pressing with steam.)

2. Place the pieced unit on the pressing surface with the piece that will lie on top of the seam allowances facing

you as shown in the illustration below. Set the stitches by pressing the seam allowances flat for a few seconds to help stitches sink into the fabric and press out any minor puckering in the seamline. (Big puckers must be eliminated by removing the stitches and reassembling the unit.)

3. Use your fingertips and the point of the iron to direct and press the patch on the top of the unit so that it lies smooth and flat over the seam allowances. Remember the pressing mantra: Lower, press, lift, lower, press, lift. *Don't slide the iron.*

4. Flip over the unit and press from the wrong side, too.

SET THE STITCHES in the seamline. Press the darker patch toward the seam allowances.

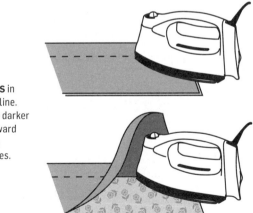

CHAPTER 3

MAKING PATCHWORK BLOCKS

In this chapter, you'll learn how to piece several basic patchwork units to create blocks. We'll begin with the traditional Log Cabin block shown on the cover to practice cutting squares and rectangles from strips and sewing them together. These are the most basic patch shapes, and you will use them in many other block designs. Making Log Cabin blocks will give you lots of practice with basic piecing.

Many of the most-used patchwork blocks are constructed with some combination of squares, rectangles, or triangles. After the Log Cabin block, you'll find directions for making nine other basic patchwork blocks that use these shapes. You will also learn additional piecing methods, including two ways to cut and piece both of the most basic triangle units used in quilt blocks — half-square triangles and quarter-square triangles.

If you sew along as you read and learn how to piece each sampler block shown in the following pages, you will have nine different finished blocks to make the Beginner's Sampler Quilt, shown on page 114. You are sure to use the techniques you learn while making these units and blocks, again and again, in other quilt projects.

What about Pinning?

Pinning small patches together for stitching isn't usually necessary, but if you feel better with patches pinned, use only one or two long quilter's pins or flat flower-head pins per set of patches. Place the points toward the raw edges to be joined; be sure to remove them as you go or stitch very slowly when you reach them to avoid broken needles and pins, and inaccurate stitching. As you gain experience, you'll probably find pinning isn't needed for joining patches with straight edges. Quilters' cottons tend to "grab" onto each other, so shifting while stitching is generally not a problem.

When joining rows of blocks, you *will* need pins to match up and secure seamlines, as well as when sewing the rows together and adding borders to complete your quilt top.

BASIC PIECING

You can make most traditional patchwork blocks with basic piecing, following a block diagram to arrange the patches into the required block rows. Then it's a simple matter to align the raw edges and sew the pieces together in each row, using the accurate ¼"-wide seam allowance you learned about in chapter 2 and pressing as directed in your block pattern or directions. (See pages 40–41 for how to press patchwork units.) Next, you will sew the block rows together to complete the block — it's as simple as that. As always, accuracy counts, so take your time to cut and sew carefully.

ALTERNATE PIECING METHODS

Some patchwork blocks and block units that feature triangles can actually be made without cutting and handling any triangles. The Snowball block (page 64) is a good example in which you cut and use the folded-corner piecing method (pages 52 and 56) to create the triangles instead. Both methods improve accuracy and speed up your work.

The directions for the nine sampler blocks in this chapter will give you practice with basic piecing, sandwich piecing (page 54), and folded-corner piecing.

MAKING A LOG CABIN BLOCK

LET'S BEGIN WITH THE CLASSIC Log Cabin block. It has a center square surrounded by rectangles that are added in either a clockwise or counterclockwise fashion. The center square of a traditional Log Cabin block usually was red to symbolize the hearth, the heart of the home, but you can use any color you like. The surrounding rectangles represent the "logs," arranged around the square so they divide the finished block diagonally into light and dark halves. The size of the square and the width and number of surrounding rectangles varies, depending on the pattern you are following.

You can use one light print and one dark print for the rectangles in the two halves of the block, or mix it up with assorted scraps of fabrics that "read" light and dark in your chosen color scheme — for example, scraps of several different pink prints and several different brown prints surrounding a red or dark pink center square (see chapter 1 or pages 12-17).

Follow the cutting chart on page 47 to make a single block of the desired size. See Easy Log Cabin Projects on page 48 for ways to use your blocks.

STEP-BY-STEP LOG CABIN BLOCK

1. Sew the shortest light rectangle #1 to the center square and press the seam allowance toward the strip (see pressing arrows). Rotate the piece one turn *counterclockwise* and add rectangle #2. Press toward the strip as shown. (If you prefer, you can turn clockwise instead, and just keep going in the same direction for the entire block.)

2. Add the shortest dark rectangle #3, turn counterclockwise and add the next dark rectangle (#4). Press all seam allowances toward the strips after you add each one.

3. Add the remaining light rectangles and dark rectangles in numerical order, always turning counterclockwise.

ROTATE THE BLOCK counterclockwise to add each new rectangle.

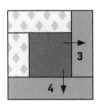

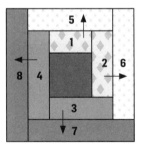

Cutting for Log Cabin Blocks

Choose the desired finished size of the block and cut one each of the pieces listed in the chart for that size.

Block	Center Square	Light Rectangles	Dark Rectangles
FINISHED SIZE	PIECE SIZE	PIECE SIZE	PIECE SIZE
6"	2½" square	**#1:** 1½" × 2½"	**#3:** 1½" × 3½"
		#2: 1½" × 3½"	**#4:** 1½" × 4½"
		#5: 1½" × 4½"	**#6:** 1½" × 5½"
		#7: 1½" × 5½"	**#8:** 1½" × 6½"
9"	3½" square	**#1:** 2" × 3½"	**#3:** 2" × 5"
		#2: 2" × 5"	**#4:** 2" × 6½"
		#5: 2" × 6½"	**#6:** 2" × 8"
		#7: 2" × 8"	**#8:** 2" × 9½"
12"	4½" square	**#1:** 2½" × 4½"	**#3:** 2½" × 6½"
		#2: 2½" × 6½"	**#4:** 2½" × 8½"
		#5: 2½" × 8½"	**#6:** 2½" × 10½"
		#7: 2½" × 10½"	**#8:** 2½" × 12½"

Easy Log Cabin Projects

Make practice blocks in the desired size for one or more of the projects described below. To make "scrappy" blocks, choose fat quarters (18" × 22" pre-cuts) of three different light prints and three different dark prints in the desired color scheme, instead of choosing only one light and one dark print.

- A 9"-square Log Cabin block makes a great pot holder when you layer it with batting and backing, quilt it, and bind it as directed in chapter 5.

- For a set of four 14½" × 18" Log Cabin placemats, make four 12"-square Log Cabin blocks following the chart on page 47. Cut and stitch 1½" × 12½" border strips in a coordinating color to the top and bottom opposite edges of each completed

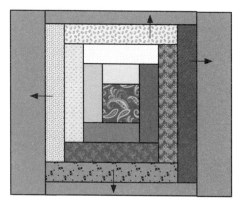

ADD STRIPS to all sides for a placemat.

block. Press seam allowances toward the borders. Then cut and add 3¼" × 14" strips to the remaining raw edges; press. Layer, quilt, and bind as you would a quilt (see chapter 5).

- Make twenty-five 6"-square Log Cabin blocks and arrange them into five rows of five blocks each to make a 30"-square quilt top. Refer to chapter 4 for directions on sewing them together and cutting and adding borders (cut fabric strips 3¼" wide for a small quilt that finishes to 36" square). Log Cabin blocks offer lots of quilt design possibilities because you can twist and turn them, row by row, to alter the placement of the light and dark halves, creating interesting secondary patterns. For inspiration, look for Log Cabin quilt designs online or in books at your local quilt shop.

Chain Piecing

When you are making several blocks all the same size, you can use *chain piecing* to streamline block assembly. You'll save time and thread with this method. Rather than finishing one block at a time, piece identical units for all blocks in one big batch — don't stop sewing to clip threads, and remove just-joined patches or units from the machine before stitching the next one. This method is great for piecing several Log Cabin blocks at once. Fourpatch blocks (page 58) are made of many two-patch units that you can chain-piece in a batch to speed up the stitching and pressing. You can also use chain piecing when joining units to complete blocks, for example when sewing sets of two-patch units together to make lots of Fourpatch blocks or units.

1. Align the raw edges of two patches and use a pin or two to hold them together. Prepare all other similar patch sets in the same way. Stack the units to the left of the presser foot with the pinned edges parallel to the presser-foot edge.

2. Stitch the first pair of patches together, stitching off the edge of the fabric for a stitch or two; this will make a tiny thread chain. Without lifting the presser foot, position the next set of patches and feed it under the toes of the presser foot and keep on stitching. Continue in this manner until you have sewn the seam in all the prepared units, making a little "clothesline" of patches.

3. At the ironing board, snip the thread chains to release each one. Press as directed in your quilt pattern.

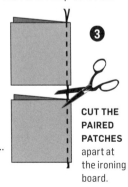

3

CUT THE PAIRED PATCHES apart at the ironing board.

PIECING BASIC TRIANGLE UNITS

TRIANGLES ARE USED IN MANY of the most common patchwork blocks. The strong angled lines add visual interest and natural divisions for using a variety of fabrics in a block. The half-square triangle and the quarter-square triangle are the most-used pieced-triangle units. Refer to chapter 2 for guidance on cutting the necessary pieces.

Piecing Half-Square Triangles

When making only a few half-square triangles, Method 1 is quick, but you must take care when handling and joining the long bias edges to avoid stretching. To avoid bias edges completely, use Method 2.

METHOD 1: TRADITIONALLY PIECED HALF-SQUARE TRIANGLES

Cut squares for this unit $7/8$" larger than the desired finished size. For example, if the finished unit or block should be 4" square, cut the squares for the triangles $4\frac{7}{8}$" × $4\frac{7}{8}$".

1. Rotary-cut two squares of different colors to the desired size. Cut each in half diagonally.

2. Align the long bias edges of two triangles of different colors. Stitch together with a $\frac{1}{4}$"-wide seam. Press the seam allowances toward the darker triangle in the finished unit and trim away the seam-allowance points that extend beyond the edges of the resulting square. Repeat to make two.

(continued on next page)

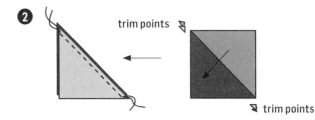

METHOD 2: FOLDED-CORNER PIECING

It's easy to make accurate units with this method, but there is some waste. For other ways to use this technique, see Cut-No-Triangles Folded-Corner Piecing, page 55.

1. Cut squares from each of two different-color fabrics to the desired finished size plus ½" for seam allowances. For example, for a 3" finished unit, cut 3½" squares.

2. With a sharp pencil, draw a diagonal line from corner to corner on the wrong side of the lighter-color square.

3. With right sides together and raw edges aligned, stitch on the drawn line.

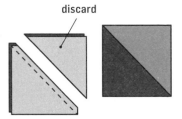

4. Trim ¼" from the stitching and discard the cutaway triangles or save them for your scrap box.

Piecing Quarter-Square Triangles

With both of the following methods, accurate cutting, marking, and stitching are essential. With each method, you will have enough triangles to make two Hourglass units (below).

METHOD 1: TRADITIONALLY PIECED QUARTER-SQUARE TRIANGLES

This technique may be easier for beginners. Cut squares 1¼" larger than the desired finished size. Take care not to stretch the bias edges as you assemble the unit (or an Hourglass block).

1. Cut an equal number of squares of the size specified in the pattern you are following and cut each one in half twice diagonally as shown on page 30.

2. Sew triangles together in sets of two, press the seam allowances in opposing directions, and then sew them together, matching the intersecting seamlines (page 60). Handle the triangles carefully to avoid stretching them out of shape. Press and trim away the seam points.

SEW QUARTER-SQUARE triangles together.

Hourglass unit

METHOD 2: SANDWICH-PIECED QUARTER-SQUARE TRIANGLES

With this method, you avoid handling bias-cut edges. You will need a ¼" presser foot for your sewing machine. For quarter-square triangles, the squares you will start with are cut 1¼" larger than the desired finished size of the unit; when following a pattern, that amount has already been added to the desired finished size to determine the strip width to cut.

1. Cut squares of the specified size in the pattern you are following from each of two fabrics. Draw a diagonal line from corner to corner on the wrong side of the lighter square.

2. With right sides together, place a lighter square on a darker square, with raw edges aligned. Stitch a scant ¼" from the line on both sides.

3. Cut on the drawn line, creating two half-square-triangle units. Press the seam toward the darker color in each one. Place the units side by side, with the colors and seamlines positioned as shown on the facing page.

4. Flip the right-hand unit facedown on the left one and nestle the diagonal seamlines together; if the seamlines are snugly nested, the raw edges around the square may not match precisely, but don't worry about that. Draw a diagonal line *across the seamline* from corner to corner. Stitch ¼" from the line on each side and cut on the drawn line for two quarter-square triangles units. Press.

5. Measure the finished unit. It may be a bit larger than the desired finished size, including ¼" seam allowances all around. Carefully trim away the excess on each edge of the square, taking care to keep the X centered in the trimmed square. For example, for a 6½" square, trim so the center X of the block is 3¼" from each outer edge.

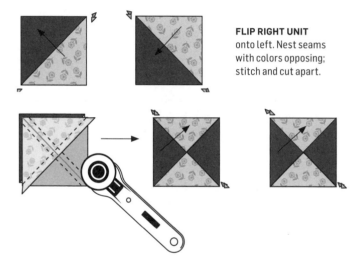

FLIP RIGHT UNIT
onto left. Nest seams
with colors opposing;
stitch and cut apart.

CUT-NO-TRIANGLES FOLDED-CORNER PIECING

Because of their bias edges and sharp points, triangle patches with bias edges are a bit challenging to match to other patches for accurate stitching. With the ingenious folded-corner-piecing method, you add small triangles to one or more corners of a square or rectangle without cutting any triangles; instead you use squares and a method similar to sandwich piecing (see page 54). It's fast and accurate and avoids dealing with the stretch along bias edges. There is some fabric waste with this method, but its speed and accuracy make it a popular technique. You will use it to make several of the basic blocks that follow.

EASY FOLDED-CORNER PIECING

1. Cut small squares and a larger square or rectangle as specified in the cutting directions for the block you are making. Draw a diagonal line from corner to corner on the wrong side of each small square.

2. Position the small square on the larger square with the drawn line in the direction shown. Stitch on the line and cut away the corner of both fabrics ¼" from the stitching. Press the resulting small triangle toward the seam allowances (unless otherwise directed).

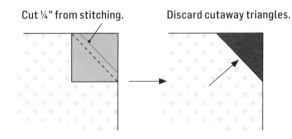

Cut ¼" from stitching.   Discard cutaway triangles.

MAKING THE SAMPLER BLOCKS

IT'S TIME TO PRACTICE MAKING blocks. Choose two fabrics you love in two contrasting colors — a light or medium-light print and a darker one. (If you want to use your practice blocks to make a small quilt, choose and purchase fabrics as directed in the Beginner's Sampler Quilt on page 114.)

Before you begin, prepare your sewing machine as directed in chapter 1 (page 9). Refer to chapter 2 as you cut, sew, and press to make each block. Follow the cutting and piecing directions for each block. Make sure you know how to sew an accurate ¼"-wide patchwork seam (pages 32–33) and use

....

Using the Sampler Blocks

Make the nine sampler blocks shown on the folowing pages to hone your quiltmaking skills and use them to make the Beginner's Sampler Quilt shown on page 114. It's the perfect size for a small wall hanging or table topper. Each block finishes to a 6"-square block (6½" square before joining into the quilt top). The blocks are joined in a straight setting (page 115) with rows of sashing and cornerstones between the blocks to frame them.

If you prefer, you can use your practice blocks for small projects (such as pot holders or placemats) or put them aside for reference when making other blocks. If you have a favorite block in the set of nine, make multiples of it to use in a straight setting with alternating plain squares for a quilt top (see page 76).

....

it throughout the block and quilt-top assembly. Several of the blocks have multiples of a single unit; practice chain piecing (page 50) when making them, to save time and thread.

FOURPATCH BLOCK

1. Cut one 3½" × 8" strip each of light and of dark fabric. From each strip, crosscut two 3½" squares.

2. Make 2 two-patch units; press seam allowances toward the darker square in each one.

3. Arrange units with seamlines nestled into each other. Pin at the seamlines as directed in Matching Intersecting Seamlines (page 60). Sew the units together. Press seam allowances as directed.

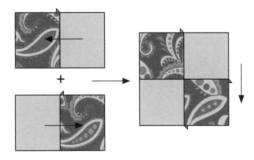

JOIN 2 two-patch units.

1. Cut one 2½" × 14" strip each of light and of dark fabric. From the light strip, crosscut four 2½" light squares. Crosscut five 2½" dark squares.

2. Arrange the squares in three rows, checkerboard style. Sew them together in rows. Press the seam allowances toward the darker color square(s) in each row.

3. Join the rows, carefully matching the seams; use a pin at each set of intersecting seamlines to hold them in place (see Matching Intersecting Seamlines on the next page). Stitch. Press the seam allowances as directed.

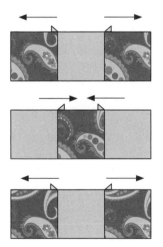

PRESS THE SEAMS in opposing directions, row to row.

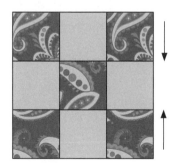

Matching Intersecting Seamlines

When blocks are made of rows with more than one patch in the row, there will be seamlines to match when the rows are joined. For this reason, patchwork seam allowances are pressed in opposing directions from row to row to make it easier to position the seamlines that must match. With seam allowances pressed in opposite directions, it's easy to align and pin them for stitching.

1. Nest the opposing seams and pin together by inserting a pin through each seam allowance. Place them perpendicular to the seamline as shown, or angle a single pin so that it catches each set of seam allowances.

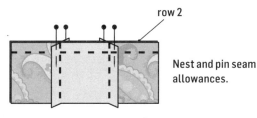

row 2

Nest and pin seam allowances.

row 1

2. Carefully stitch one or two stitches past the intersecting seam-lines *before removing the pin* (counter to what you've been taught about sewing over pins), but sew slowly or use the machine's hand wheel to avoid hitting the pins with the machine needle. Whenever possible, stitch with the seam allowances that are pressed toward you on the bottom so the feed dogs won't push them out of position. You can prevent this by controlling the top seam allowances with the point of your seam ripper, a straight pin, or a bamboo skewer to keep the presser foot from moving them out of position. The pins also help control the seam allowances.

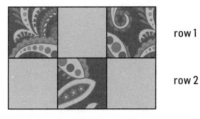

row 1

row 2

+

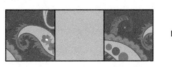

row 3

TWO-BY-TWO BLOCK

1. Cut one 2" × 16" strip each of light and of dark fabric. From each strip, crosscut four 2" × 3½" rectangles.

2. Sew light and dark rectangles together in pairs to make four two-patch units. Press the seams toward the darker rectangle.

3. Join units in two rows of two each; press as directed. Sew together, carefully matching the center seam, and press.

MAKE 4 units.

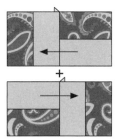

JOIN units in 2 rows.

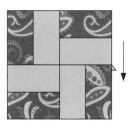

STITCH the rows together.

TAM'S PATCH BLOCK (VARIATION)

1. Cut one 2" × 14" strip each of light and of dark fabrics. Cut two 2" squares from each strip and two 2" × 3½" rectangles from each strip. Cut one 3⅞" square from the light and from the dark fabrics; cut each square in half diagonally.

2. With right sides together and raw edges aligned, sew each light triangle to a dark triangle, taking care not to stretch the long bias edges while stitching. Press and trim as shown on page 52. Make 2 half-square triangle units.

3. Make 2 two-patch units with the 2" light and dark squares; press seam allowances toward the dark squares. Arranging as shown, sew each unit to a 2" × 3½" dark rectangle to make 2 three-patch units. Press as directed.

4. Arrange the three-patch and half-square-triangle units in two rows as shown; sew them together and press as directed. Sew the rows together and press.

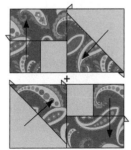

make 2

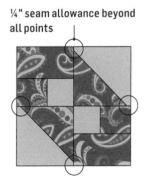

¼" seam allowance beyond all points

SNOWBALL BLOCK

Traditionally, you would need a template to cut the large center patch for this popular block, and you would cut two small squares in half for the four triangles. But that's not necessary with folded-corner piecing (see page 56).

1. Cut one 2½" × 12" light strip; crosscut four 2½" light squares from it. Cut one 6½" dark square.

2. Use a sharp pencil and a 6"-square acrylic ruler to draw a diagonal line from corner to corner on the wrong side of each 2½" light square. Position the marked squares at each corner of the large square with the line intersecting adjacent edges.

3. Stitch on each line. Trim ¼" outside each stitching line and press each small triangle toward the seam allowances.

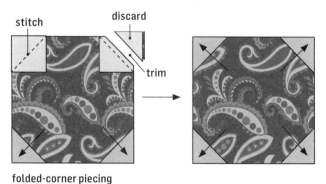

folded-corner piecing

FLYING GEESE BLOCK

This unit is traditionally pieced by sewing two small triangles to a larger one, but use the folded-corner piecing method (pages 52 and 56) instead for perfect "geese" every time!

1. Cut one 3½" × 16" light strip; crosscut four 3½" light squares. Cut one 3½" × 14" dark strip; crosscut two 3½" × 6½" dark rectangles.

2. Draw a diagonal line from corner to corner on the wrong side of each of the four light squares.

3. Position one square at the left-hand end of a rectangle. Stitch on the diagonal line and then trim ¼" from the stitching (a). Press (b). Repeat with another light square and the remaining dark rectangle.

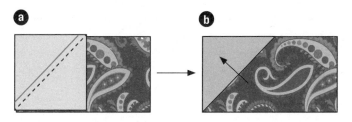

(continued on next page)

4. Repeat with the other squares at the opposite end of the two rectangles, noting the position of the line in the illustrations below. The result is a Flying Geese unit. Note how the point ends ¼" below the cut edge of the unit so you can sew units together to make a Flying Geese block without cutting off the "beak of the goose."

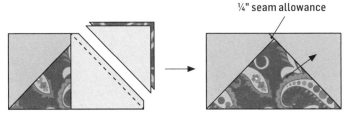

¼" seam allowance

make 2

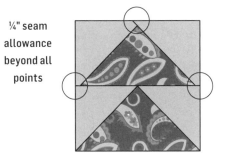

¼" seam allowance beyond all points

SQUARE-IN-A-SQUARE BLOCK

1. Cut one 3½" × 16" light strip; crosscut four 3½" light squares. Cut one 6½" dark square.

2. Draw a diagonal line from corner to corner on the wrong side of each small light square. Position two small squares in opposite corners of the larger dark square, with the drawn lines intersecting adjacent edges. Stitch on the lines. Trim ¼" from the stitching and press the resulting small triangles toward the seam allowances.

3. Repeat in the other corners with the remaining small triangles. Note how the point ends ¼" below the cut edge of the unit so you can sew units together without cutting points off in the seams.

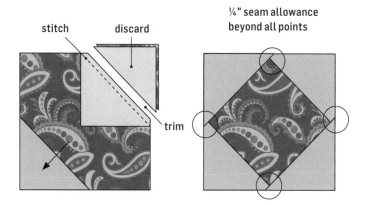

HOURGLASS BLOCK

1. Cut one 7¼" square each of light and of dark fabric. Layer the squares with raw edges aligned; cut twice diagonally for four triangles of each (see page 30). You will have enough triangles to make two blocks.

2. Follow the directions for traditionally pieced quarter-square triangles on page 53 to complete the block.

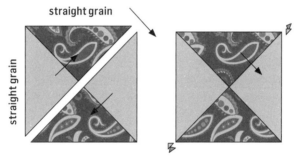

JOIN 2 quarter-square triangle units.

PINWHEEL BLOCK

Making the half-square triangles for this block is easy. The challenge is in accurately joining the intersecting points (see page 70).

1. Cut one 3½" × 15" strip each of light and of dark fabric. Crosscut four 3½" squares from each strip. Follow the directions for folded-corner piecing on page 52 to make four half-square triangle units.

2. Arrange the units in rows of two, paying attention to triangle/color placement as shown in the illustration. Sew the units together in rows and press the seam allowances in opposing directions, so it will be easy to match seamlines.

3. Position the finished rows, again checking the color placement so a pinwheel forms. Turn the upper row facedown on the lower row. Snug the center seamlines into each other and pin the seamline intersection as shown in Matching Intersecting Points on the next page to avoid nipping off the triangle points in the seamline. Sew together.

4. Press the seam allowances in one direction or, if you prefer, press the center seam open for a flatter seam at the point where all four diagonal seamlines meet in the finished block.

make 4

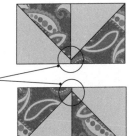

¼" seam allowance beyond points

JOIN HALF-SQUARE-triangle units in 2 rows.

Matching Intersecting Points

Joining units with two intersecting points offers a piecing challenge that is easy to handle if you learn to "stitch for the X."

1. Press so the seam allowances oppose each other. This might mean changing the direction that a seam was originally pressed — and that may create a twist in the seam on the wrong side of the unit. That's okay.

2. To align the points, place the pieces right sides together and insert a pin at the seamline on the wrong side of the unit on top. Shift the lower unit so you can see the point of the pin and insert it into the bottom unit. Bring the point back through the top unit so the pinhead is against the top layer.

3. Insert a pin on each side of the matching point to securely hold the pieces in place while stitching. When you reach the pinned area, stitch *slowly* over the pin and across the intersection. Aim for the X formed by the stitching and err in favor of the point by stitching a thread or two away from it, in the seam allowance, so you don't nip off the point in the stitching. Complete the seam.

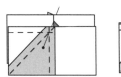

PIERCE seamlines at points.

PIN seam allowances.

AIM for the × when stitching the seam.

CHAPTER 4

ASSEMBLING THE QUILT TOP

When you've completed the blocks for your project, you're ready to sew them together to make the quilt top (or to turn a single block into a small project of your choice). Most quilts have two or more rows of two or more blocks. The arrangement of the blocks is called the *quilt setting*. If you are following a pattern, the setting was determined by the designer.

EASY QUILT SETTINGS

THE TWO MOST COMMON QUILT SETTINGS are straight and diagonal. We'll stick to straight settings in this book; diagonal settings are a bit more challenging. They are dynamic and interesting and something to explore in future projects, when you have a bit more experience.

In the traditional straight setting, blocks are placed side by side with other blocks or alternating plain squares and sewn together to create rows. Then the block rows are sewn together to complete the quilt top. The simplest version of this setting combines pieced squares with alternating plain squares. This setting makes it faster to create a quilt top because only half of the squares are pieced. It's easier, too, because when you join pieced squares to plain ones, there are no seam intersections to match (as there would be when joining pieced squares to

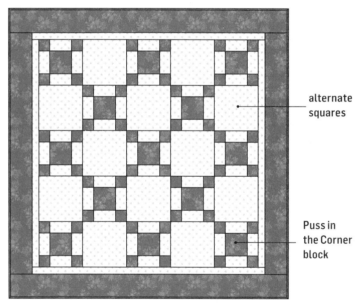

alternate squares

Puss in the Corner block

STRAIGHT SETTING with alternating squares: Puss in the Corner blocks alternate with plain squares, resulting in a Single Irish Chain quilt.

each other, side by side). As an example, when you alternate Puss in the Corner blocks with plain squares, the result is the traditional Single Irish Chain quilt design (facing page).

When you alternate two pieced blocks, side by side, and then row to row, you can create interesting secondary patterns as shown in this nine-block arrangement of Sawtooth Stars and Snowballs. Blocks with triangles in the outer corners, such as Snowball (page 64) and Square-in-a-Square (page 67), or with squares in the outer corners, such as Puss in the Corner (facing page), are some popular choices for this type of setting.

Sawtooth Star —

Snowball —

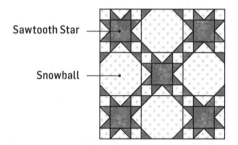

STRAIGHT SETTING with pieced blocks: When corners of two different pieced blocks connect, a new pattern emerges.

The straight setting with sashing is an easy variation. The blocks in each horizontal row are joined with vertical sashing strips, and then the block rows are sewn together with horizontal sashing strips connected with cornerstones. This setting is often used in sampler quilts, where each block is different, to create a frame around each one that allows it to sparkle on its own. It's easy because there are no block seams to match when you join the blocks into rows. The Beginner's Sampler Quilt (page 114) features a sashed setting.

Preparing and Arranging the Blocks

Before you arrange the blocks in any setting, follow these steps to get them ready:

1. Turn each block to the wrong side and trim any thread tails close to the outer raw edges and seam allowance edges. If left on the wrong side, these threads will show through light-colored fabrics in your quilt blocks, creating a visual distraction. Also remove any stray threads on the block surface.

2. Check all seam allowances and make sure they are pressed flat on the wrong side of the block. If you find some accidentally twisted seam allowances, it's not necessary to undo and restitch them; press them as flat as possible on the wrong side and press from the right side as needed. Use a dry iron; too much steam can distort your carefully pieced blocks.

3. Check the finished blocks to make sure they are the same size. Use your rotary cutting tools to square them up. A large square rotary ruler is handy for this step. *All blocks should measure ½" larger all around than the finished block size specified in your pattern.* For example, a 9" finished block should measure 9½" square. If there are any blocks that are way off in size, take the time to make a new block if you have enough fabric to do so. It's easier and less time-consuming than trying to adjust seams in small pieces. If you don't have fabric for a new block,

carefully undo stitching and repair the block. Be careful not to stretch bias edges on the patches.

4. Follow the pattern directions to cut any setting pieces you need, such as plain squares or sashing strips and cornerstones.

5. Refer to your quilt pattern directions to arrange the blocks (and setting squares or sashing and cornerstone pieces, if applicable) on a large flat surface. This puts them in ready-to-sew position.

Sewing the Blocks and Rows Together

After arranging all the blocks and setting pieces and labeling the rows as directed in Keeping the Pieces Organized (below), get ready to sew and press. Choose the appropriate directions from those on the following pages for the setting style you are using.

Keeping the Pieces Organized

When there are a number of pieces in each row, label the blocks and rows to keep them in order at the machine. After arranging the blocks in rows, label each block with its row number and position. Work from left to right as in 1A, 1B, 1C, etc., write the numbers on small pieces of paper, and pin each one in the upper left-hand quadrant of the blocks. Placing labels in the left upper corner helps identify the orientation of the blocks in each row.

STRAIGHT SETTING ASSEMBLY

1. Sew the blocks together in each horizontal row of the layout, carefully matching and pinning any intersecting seamlines as you learned for block assembly (see page 61). When joining pieced blocks to pieced blocks, you may need to repress or twist one or more pressed seam allowances in the opposite direction so the seamlines will nest into each other for a perfect match.

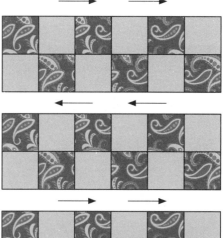

STRAIGHT SETTING: Press each row in opposite directions.

2. Press the seam allowances in opposite directions from row to row so the intersecting seamlines will nest into each other when joining rows. However, if you are joining pieced blocks with alternating plain squares or pieced blocks with fewer seams (a Snowball or Puss in the Corner block, for example), press the seam allowances toward the alternate squares or pieced blocks with fewer seams. That's the direction the seam allowances will want to go anyway.

3. Joining two rows at a time, use as many pins as you need to hold the block rows together for seam matching and smooth seaming. When rows are joined in pairs, sew the pairs together, adding the remaining odd-numbered row if there is one. Press all the seam allowances toward the bottom edge of the quilt top.

STRAIGHT SASHED SETTING ASSEMBLY

For each step, *press all seam allowances toward the sashing strips* to position them in opposing directions for easy row-to-row matching. (See the pressing arrows in the illustrations.)

1. Arrange the blocks and vertical sashing strips together in horizontal rows; sew together and press.

2. Arrange the remaining sashing strips with the cornerstones in horizontal rows. Sew together and press.

3. Arrange the block rows with the sashing/cornerstone strips in alternating fashion on your work surface. With right sides together and the sashing/cornerstone strip on the bottom, pin the first sashing/cornerstone row to the upper edge of the first block row. Carefully match and nest the seamlines at the intersections of the sashing and cornerstones. Sew, removing pins as you reach them and keeping the block seam allowances in position as you sew. After completing a seam, flip to the sashing side and check the stitching and seam accuracy; correct as needed. Press the seam allowances toward the sashing strip.

4. Continue in this manner to add the remaining sashing/cornerstone and block rows in alternating fashion. Press all seam allowances toward the sashing rows.

sashing row

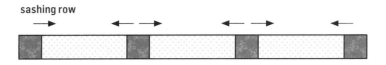

block row

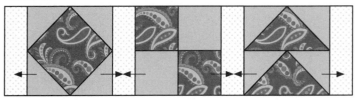

STRAIGHT SASHED SETTING: Press all seam allowances toward the sashing.

CUTTING AND ADDING BORDERS

A BORDER ACTS LIKE A FRAME around your quilt top: it stops the viewer's eye and draws it back to the blocks, where you've put all your work. Borders also add space to show off a special quilted design, adding more visual appeal. Some quilts have multiple borders, pieced borders, or appliquéd borders, but we'll stick to adding only one border with straight-cut corners. (For multiple borders, however, you simply repeat the basic steps for measuring, cutting, and adding a single border.) Modern quilters often avoid adding borders entirely, finishing the quilt top with binding only.

For your border, choose one of the fabrics you've used in the blocks of your quilt or one that coordinates with all of the other fabrics. It should complement and set off the blocks, not compete with them. When following someone else's pattern, examine the sample quilt photo and follow the designer's lead for fabric choices. Don't copy it precisely; just look for similar fabric types in a color palette you like and in the values shown.

Measuring accurately and cutting carefully are essential when adding borders so the resulting quilt is "square and true." The side borders must be cut the same length, even if the measurements at the outer edges of the quilt top do not match. Otherwise, one edge of the finished quilt will be shorter than the other, creating a lopsided quilt. The same is true for the top and bottom borders.

STEP-BY-STEP BORDERS

1. Press the finished quilt top and then smooth it out on a flat, firm surface. Use a long ruler or a tape measure to measure the length through the center (see illustration on page 82).

2. Use rotary cutting tools to cut two border strips the desired or specified width by the length measurement from step 1. Cut the required number of border strips across the width of the border fabric, unless otherwise directed in the pattern. If the border measurement is greater than 40" of usable width, you will cut additional strips as needed and join them into one long strip as described in Joining Strips with Diagonal Seams (page 83).

3. Once the border strips are the desired length, fold each in half crosswise and mark the center with a pin or water- or air-soluble marker on the right side. Repeat with the quilt top.

4. With right sides together, place a border strip on one edge of the quilt top; pin and match centers and ends. Pin the block seam allowances in place as needed to keep the long raw edges aligned. Pin the other border to the opposite edge in the same way.

(continued on next page)

5. With the quilt top and pins facing you, sew ¼" from the raw edges, removing the pins as you reach them. Secure the stitches at the beginning and end of the seam with backstitching. Press the borders away from the quilt top, toward the seam allowances. (*Note:* If your quilt top has sashing/cornerstone strips, press the seam allowances toward the sashing instead.)

6. Repeat steps 1 and 2 to measure the quilt-top width through the center and cut two border strips (join strips if necessary) to match that measurement. Mark, pin, stitch, and press as directed for the first two borders in steps 3–5. With the borders in place, you are ready to finish, quilt, and bind your project (see chapter 5).

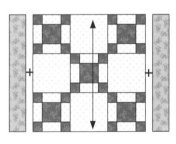
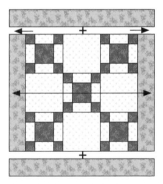

MEASURE THROUGH THE CENTER for accurate borders. Add side borders first, followed by top and bottom borders

Joining Strips with Diagonal Seams

Use this technique when joining strips to make them long enough for quilt borders and binding strips (page 107). Using diagonal seams helps distribute the bulk of the seam allowances along the seams, and they aren't as noticeable in the finished border or binding as end-to-end straight joins are.

1. Place two strips right sides together at a perfect right (90-degree) angle. Use the grid on the cutting mat to help with alignment. Place a ruler diagonally at the strip edges where they intersect and draw a stitching line at a 45-degree angle with a sharp pencil. *Do not cut on this line*.

2. Remove the ruler. Without moving the strips, place one or two pins across the line through both fabric layers; stitch on the line. Trim the excess ¼" outside the stitching line. Repeat to make one long strip to the required length. Press the seams open.

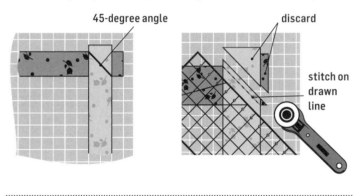

45-degree angle

discard

stitch on drawn line

CHAPTER 5

FINISHING YOUR QUILT

When your quilt top is completed, you are ready to turn it into a quilt. First, you create a "quilt sandwich" with the quilt top, batting, and backing, and then you baste the layers together for machine quilting. After completing the quilting, you will bind the outer edges of the quilt to finish it. And, finally, you'll add a label to the back to document your work.

PREPARING THE QUILT TOP

To ENSURE SUCCESSFUL RESULTS, don't skip this all-important step.

1. Clip all stray threads on the back of the quilt so they won't show through light-colored patches on the front.

2. Press any seam allowances that are not smooth and flat. If there are any twisted seam allowances, make sure the twisted area is pressed as flat as possible.

3. Press the right side as needed. Look for seamlines that are not lying smooth and flat. Eliminate any wrinkles in the patches, continuing the up-and-down pressing motion you learned when making blocks (see pages 38–41). Use light steam as needed.

4. Make sure all four corners are true and square. Square up with rotary cutting tools as required.

5. Read about and prepare the batting as described on page 21.

MAKING THE QUILT SANDWICH

To MAKE A QUILT SANDWICH, you need the finished patchwork top with borders attached, plus batting and backing. Work on your cutting table, a kitchen counter, the top of your dryer, or even on the floor if necessary — any large, flat area will do. If you belong to a church or other organization, you may be able to set up a time to use their long rectangular tables for layering large quilts.

STEP-BY-STEP QUILT SANDWICH

Refer to the illustration on page 88 for the following steps.

1. Cut a piece of backing fabric at least 2" larger all around than the size of a small quilt top, or at least 1" larger all around for small projects such as a pot holder, pillow cover, or placemat. For projects larger than 38" wide, make a backing 6" to 8" larger all around with two or more panels of fabric as detailed in How to Piece a Backing (page 89). Make sure the backing panel is wrinkle-free.

2. Use your hands to smooth out wrinkles and creases in the quilt batting before cutting it the same size as the backing.

3. Find the center of each edge of the backing and mark with water- or air-soluble marker on the wrong side.

Also find the center of each edge of the batting and the quilt top and mark on the right side of each.

4. Place the backing right side down on your work surface. Beginning at each center mark, work to the outer corners of each edge and keep the backing taut, but not stretched while you secure it to the work surface with small pieces of masking tape. It must be smooth and flat on the work surface, with square corners in order to avoid lots of undesirable "tucks" in the quilt backing after you have quilted it.

5. Place the batting on top of the backing, aligning centers. Smooth in place from the center out; it's not necessary to tape it. Don't worry if the raw edges don't align precisely.

6. Place the quilt top, right side up, on top of the batting with centers aligned. Make sure the top is squarely positioned on the batting/backing layers with true, square corners. Use a long ruler and a large square ruler to check, paying attention to the outer corners; do not stretch them out of "square." All horizontal seamlines should be straight and parallel to each other, and perpendicular to those running in the opposite direction. The vertical seamlines must be parallel to each other, too, and perpendicular to the horizontal ones. *Take your time to get this right;* accuracy here will have a profound effect on the appearance of the finished quilt.

(continued on next page)

7. Baste the layers together using pins or glue as outlined in Baste It! on page 91.

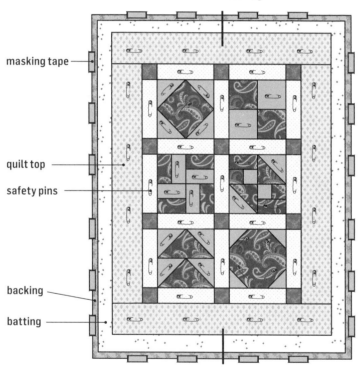

centers matching

masking tape

quilt top

safety pins

backing

batting

centers matching

The Backing

Some patterns provide the backing dimensions; others do not. For projects that measure more than 38" in either direction, you will need to sew panels together to make a backing of the required size. For larger projects, up to 54" wide, the backing should measure at least 6" larger around. For bed-size and larger quilts, add 8" to the quilt-top dimensions to determine the backing size.

Although there are other ways to piece backings, the following is one is the most commonly used. Refer to *The Quilting Answer Book* (see Resources and Links on page 118) for more options for making pieced backings. We will use a 54"-square quilt top as the example in the following steps.

HOW TO PIECE A BACKING

1. Determine the required backing size; in this example, it's 60" square (54" + 6").

2. Divide the required width by 40" (the usable width of most quilters' cottons after preshrinking). Round up to the nearest full number for the number of panels to cut. Most quilts require at least two, some three. For this example we need two 40"-wide panels (60" ÷ 40" = 1.5, rounded up to 2). Each one should be the length of the quilt top, plus the extra 6" you need. Trim the selvages from the long edges of each panel.

(continued on next page)

3. Cut one panel in half lengthwise and sew a narrow panel to each long edge of the remaining full panel with ¼"-wide seam allowances. Press the seam allowances toward the center panel.

4. Trim the resulting panel to the required width (60" in this example), making sure to center the middle panel. You can cut a hanging sleeve (page 105) from backing cutaways, or store the fabric excess in your stash.

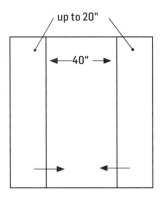

A TRIPLE-PANEL backing can be any length and up to 80" wide.

Baste It!

Basting with safety pins is the method most recommended for machine-quilting. You can also glue-baste the layers with temporary spray adhesive, which is done while you make the quilt sandwich.

PIN BASTING

Use 1" or 1½" curved, rustproof, brass- or nickel-plated pins designed especially for quilters. The curve makes it easier to maneuver the pins through the quilt layers, including the backing, which is anchored to the work surface with tape. You will need lots of pins for a large quilt. Buy them in quantity to keep secreted away for quilting only.

Open all pins before you begin; I recommend leaving them open when you remove and store them later so they are ready for the next project. As an alternative on small projects, use flat flower-head straight pins to secure the layers for machine quilting.

Work on one quarter of the project at a time and place safety pins in a grid, positioning them no more than 4" to 6" apart (about a hand's width). *Note*: You may place pins in the borders and sashing as well as in the block patches, as shown in the quilt illustration on page 88.

Insert the pins through all three layers of the quilt sandwich and then bring the point back to the quilt top. As much as possible, keep the pins away from the long horizontal or vertical seamlines if you plan to quilt-in-the-ditch (stitch in the seamlines; see page 97). You will have to remove any pins that are in the way of your quilting process as you machine-stitch, so don't place them right where you know you will be quilting. Don't close the pins until you have all of them in the right place, adjusting the position of any that need it before closing them.

GLUE BASTING

For glue basting, use temporary spray adhesive to hold the quilt-sandwich layers together. It's a quick-and-easy method for basting small projects that fit on your cutting surface or countertop.

Glue basting allows for repositioning as needed before you start stitching, and it dissipates over time — or you can remove it right away by laundering your finished quilt. Of course this means that you must preshrink your fabrics before cutting and assembling the quilt top, and you must like the appearance of laundered quilts. They have a more puckered, slightly "worn" look, much like that of antique and vintage quilts. For wall hangings, this laundered, vintage look is probably not appropriate, but consider it for lap- and bed-size quilts.

STEP-BY-STEP GLUE BASTING

1. Read the directions on the spray adhesive can. Work in a well-ventilated area — for example, a garage or outdoors — as well as where adhesive overspray is not a problem. You can place small projects in a box with high sides to catch overspray while applying the adhesive.

2. Prepare, position, and tape the backing to the work surface as directed in Making the Quilt Sandwich (page 86). Fold the batting in half lengthwise and apply a light mist of adhesive to the exposed half of the batting only. Position the folded batting, adhesive side up, on the backing's wrong side with the center marks matching. Roll the adhesive-coated side onto the backing, a bit at a time, smoothing it into place.

3. Fold the loose half of the batting back on itself and apply adhesive before smoothing it in place on the backing. Make sure everything is wrinkle-free; if not, lift and replace the piece as needed while you work out any wrinkles.

4. Repeat step 2 with the quilt top and you are ready to machine-quilt. If adhesive collects on the sewing machine needle, causing skipped stitches, wipe it off with a cotton ball saturated with rubbing alcohol.

QUILT IT!

MOST QUILTMAKERS HAVE A FAVORITE part of the quiltmaking process. Some love the design and fabric selection; others enjoy the fun of seeing the blocks come together into the quilt top. Still others love the actual quilting — perhaps because it means the project is nearing completion. Quilting adds another element of visual and artistic dimension to a quilt, bringing the flat layers to life as they are stitched together with simple lines of stitching or more elaborate designs. Like most quilters, you will probably discover that, when it comes to quilting your quilt, "a little more is better than not enough."

Is quilting really necessary? Absolutely — it's not a quilt until it's quilted! The batting fibers cling together, but they can and will shift and separate inside a quilt unless the layers are held together with appropriately spaced quilting stitches. Check the batting packaging and plan your quilting so the stitches are the package-recommended distance apart — it differs for different batting types. Quilts that will receive hard wear and regular laundering — lap and bed size — require more closely spaced quilting than those that will hang on the wall.

Some quilters still quilt by hand, an often time-consuming, meditative labor of love. In today's busy world, with today's specialized sewing machines, doing the quilting by machine has become the favorite method for many. However, some prefer to finish the quilt top and then pay a quilter with a long-arm machine do the layering and quilting. This frees quiltmakers to start their next quilting project!

Machine-quilting requires patience, practice, and attention to detail. Some quilting designs must be marked on the quilt top before making the quilt sandwich. However, we will concentrate on easy methods that don't require premarking. (For more on that subject, refer to *The Quilting Answer Book*; see Resources and Links on page 118.)

Quilting-in-the-ditch of existing seamlines in the quilt is one of the most common and simplest machine-quilting methods. It is often used to attach the quilt top to the batting and backing before adding more quilting in the blocks and borders; see page 97 for how-tos. Additional quilting in the blocks and borders adds beauty and dimension and can help disguise minor errors in the piecing. Other easy quilting methods include those featured in Quilting the Blocks (page 100).

When you are ready to expand your quilting skills beyond those discussed in this chapter, take a machine-quilting class at your local quilt shop. There are many methods for marking and stitching more elaborate designs, as well as for doing free-motion quilting without a presser foot and with the feed dogs lowered. All of these methods require instruction and practice.

Setting Up the Machine

1. Make sure the feed dogs are engaged. Adjust the machine for a stitch length of 6 to 10 stitches per inch.

2. Attach the ¼" quilters' presser foot or a walking foot, or engage the even-feed feature if available on the

machine. Another option is the open-toe foot, which gives you a clear view of the seamlines while stitching.

3. If possible on your machine, set the needle to stop in the needle-down position, so that stopping and pivoting when turning corners is easier. Otherwise it will be necessary to hand-lower the needle into the quilt before lifting the presser foot to pivot at corners in the block outlines and patches.

4. Some machines have a special quilting stitch that somewhat mimics the appearance of hand quilting. Check out and test available quilting stitches on your machine and choose the one you like.

5. Thread the needle with the desired thread. Choose from machine-quilting thread, all-purpose sewing thread, or, for invisible quilting stitches, use monofilament nylon or polyester thread. Use a matching- or contrasting-color, machine-quilting or all-purpose thread in the bobbin. Test different thread combinations on small quilt sandwiches made of fabric and batting scraps to see which appeals to you and works best.

6. Refer to your sewing machine manual to adjust the tension so that the top and bobbin threads lock in the center of the layers in your test. If the thread lies on the surface and there are little "freckles" of the bobbin thread showing, loosen the top tension. If the thread floats on the back of the quilt, tighten the top tension.

Quilting-in-the-Ditch

Quilting-in-the-ditch (also called *stitch-in-the-ditch*) is an essential skill to know because it is easy and can be used to quilt the blocks as well as for a process called *setting the quilt*. To quilt-in-the-ditch means to stitch right in the well of the seamline, and when you use it to set a quilt, you stitch in the well of the long horizontal and vertical seams that join the blocks, thus attaching the quilt top to the batting and backing layers. It creates a stitched grid that holds the blocks and batting in place and is all but invisible on the quilt front. You can see it on the back, however.

Setting the top makes it easier to keep the blocks "square" in the quilt top while you add more quilting within the blocks (and borders). If you don't want this stitching to remain permanently in the quilt, you can use water-soluble basting thread in the needle and bobbin and remove it by laundering, following the manufacturer's directions. Test first on a trial quilt sandwich made of batting and fabric scraps.

On a small quilt, setting the quilt may be all the quilting you need. However, quilting-in-the-ditch adds even more visual dimension when you also do it in the seamlines between some or all of the patches within each block, as well as along the border (and sashing) seamlines.

SETTING THE QUILT

Follow these steps to stitch the quilt top to the batting and backing before doing additional quilting in the blocks and borders.

1. Place the quilt sandwich under the machine needle and adjust so the needle is next to the first seamline where you wish to begin. Lower the needle through the layers in the seamline, right alongside the "ledge" created by pressing seam allowances to one side. This is called the *valley* or *well* of the seam.

2. Lower the presser foot. Draw the bobbin thread up to the surface. Grasping both threads in your left hand as you begin to stitch, lock the stitches with the stitch-locking feature on your machine, or adjust the stitch length so you use a few very short stitches in place before adjusting the stitch length for the quilting. Begin stitching.

3. *Do not stitch through the pressed seam allowances.* Jog to the opposite side of the seam when the pressed direction of the seam allowances changes at seam intersections. (You can see this in the vertical seamlines in the quilt shown on page 101.) Use your hands to gently spread the fabric along the seamline so your stitches stay in the valley of the seam.

4. When you reach the end of a long row of stitching, lock the stitches and clip the threads.

Handling Large Quilts at the Machine

When quilting lap-size and larger quilts, you will need to handle the bulk of the quilt under the arm of the sewing machine. Roll the quilt sandwich from opposite edges toward the quilt center, leaving 12" of the center unrolled. Secure the rolls with oval quilt clips or large safety pins. Quilt as desired, working from the center out to one edge, unrolling and securing as you go.

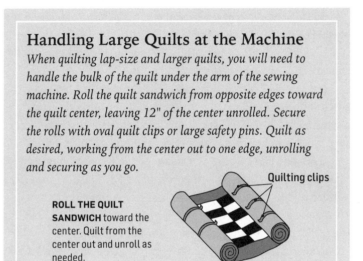

Quilting clips

ROLL THE QUILT SANDWICH toward the center. Quilt from the center out and unroll as needed.

Quilting the Blocks

For your first quilting experience, choose from the methods below. Only one requires marking on the quilt top.

Quilt-in-the-ditch of the seamlines that join the patches in the block. Follow the same procedure described in Setting the Quilt (page 98). Study the illustration (below left) for an example of this stitching in a pieced block.

Outline-quilt instead of quilting-in-the-ditch to highlight the patchwork shapes. Place the outer edge of a ¼" presser foot right along the seamline and stitch, pivoting at corners where necessary. Lock stitches at the beginning and end of the stitching.

Quilt individual blocks or a small quilt in a simple, allover grid. First set the quilt as described on page 98. Place it on a firm surface and use a ruler and chalk marker to draw guidelines at a 45-degree angle, spaced at least 1" apart in one direction across the quilt. For marking any design on your quilt top, always use a washable graphite pencil, a fine-point water- or or air-soluble

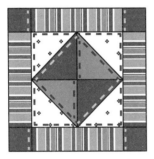

TO QUILT-IN-THE-DITCH, stitch in the "valley" of each seam.

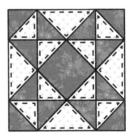

TO OUTLINE QUILT, stitch ¼" from the seamlines within some or all patches.

pen, a chalk wheel with powdered chalk, or ¼"-wide masking tape. Ask for any of these at your quilt shop and use them with a long acrylic ruler to keep lines straight and evenly spaced.

Stitch on all the lines, then draw lines in the opposite direction (at 90 degrees) and stitch. For large quilts with a grid, mark the grid in both directions on the quilt top before making the quilt sandwich. Then, quilt one quadrant (a quarter of the quilt top) at a time. This keeps the other three quadrants of the quilt to the left and above the quadrant you are quilting — lots easier to manage on the sewing machine.

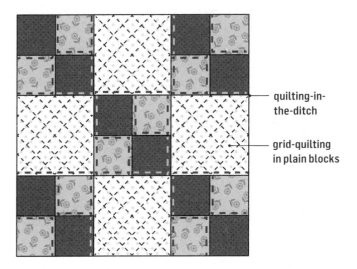

quilting-in-the-ditch

grid-quilting in plain blocks

QUILT SETTING with pieced blocks and plain alternating squares.

Quilting the Borders

To quilt the borders, the easiest solution is to quilt-in-the-ditch of the long border seams first, and then add evenly spaced rows of straight stitching within the borders and parallel to the border seams. (See the quilt illustration on page 3 for an example.) For an alternative, try a serpentine zigzag stitch, which adds visual texture and motion to the borders. Experiment with stitch width and length on a test quilt sandwich.

After choosing and adjusting the desired stitch, machine-baste a scant ¼" from the quilt-top raw edges through all quilt layers — quilt top, batting, and backing — to prevent shifting during stitching. *Don't pivot:* stitch from raw edge to raw edge and clip the threads so the corners won't pucker or draw up.

To quilt evenly spaced rows of stitching, use the edge of the presser foot as a spacing guide, *ending all quilting at least ½" to ¾" from the outer edges of the borders* so you have room for the binding seam. Begin and end the stitching in the side borders at the upper and lower border seamlines. Then quilt the top and bottom borders from raw edge to raw edge in the same manner.

Border Quilting Options

Quilt shops carry a variety of quilting stencils designed for borders, with coordinating designs for the border corners. As a beginner, look for designs with either straight lines or smooth and gentle curves. Trace along the cut lines in the borders with a removable marking method. You will need help from a more experienced quilter or teacher to choose a border stencil design and adjust it to fit the borders of your quilt before marking it on the quilt top borders.

BEFORE BINDING

With the quilting complete, you're ready for the finishing steps: adding a method to hang your quilt if you plan to do so, and finishing the raw edges with binding. It's a good idea to label your quilt, too.

Carefully trim the excess batting and backing to be even with the quilt-top edges, and make sure the corners are square. If you are making a quilted project to hang on the wall, add corner rod pockets or a hanging sleeve to the back of the quilted layers, as instructed on the following pages, before binding the quilt.

ADDING CORNER ROD POCKETS (OPTIONAL)

Corner rod pockets provide an easy way to hang a small quilt without damaging it.

1. Cut two 2" squares. Fold each one in half diagonally with wrong sides facing and raw edges even; press. Place the triangles in opposite corners at the upper edge of the quilt backing with raw edges aligned. Machine-baste in place and finish the quilt edges with binding. Do not baste the folded edge.

2. To hang, cut a ¼"- to ½"-diameter dowel that will fit under the corners. Hang the dowel on two small nails that extend from the wall to support the quilt.

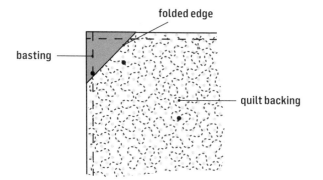

folded edge

basting

quilt backing

ADDING A HANGING SLEEVE (OPTIONAL)

A fabric sleeve on the back of your wall quilt provides a stress-free way to hang it, which is especially important for large quilts. Quilts that will be entered in competitions or hung in exhibitions must have a hanging sleeve.

1. Measure the width of the finished quilt. For small quilts, cut a 6"-wide strip of fabric 1" shorter than the width measurement; for large ones, cut it at least 8" wide (and still 1" shorter). Turn under ¼" at each short end of the strip and press; turn each end again and machine-stitch the narrow double hems in place.

2. Fold the strip in half with wrong sides facing and raw edges even but *don't press the long folded edge.* Fold the strip in half crosswise and mark the center. Fold and mark the center of the upper edge of the quilt, too.

3. Matching the centers, pin the sleeve in place on the quilt backing with the raw edges even at the upper edge of the quilt. Machine-baste in place a scant ¼" from the raw edges.

4. Use a removable marking method to draw a line on the backing along the folded lower edge of the sleeve (a) (see next page). Move the bottom edge of the sleeve ¼" above the line you drew; pin and then slipstitch in place (b).

(continued on next page)

This creates a little slack in the front of the tube to eliminate stress at the upper edge of the quilt from the quilt's weight when hanging.

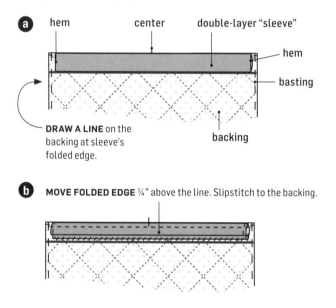

a hem ⋅ center ⋅ double-layer "sleeve" ⋅ hem ⋅ basting

DRAW A LINE on the backing at sleeve's folded edge.

backing

b **MOVE FOLDED EDGE** ¼" above the line. Slipstitch to the backing.

Remove the marked line and smooth the slack in the sleeve down, creating a new fold. Slipstitch the short ends on the back layer of the sleeve to the backing.

5. After binding the quilt (see facing page), slip a dowel through the sleeve and hang it on nails behind the quilt.

BINDING YOUR QUILT

THE MOST COMMON METHOD for finishing the outer raw edges of a quilt is with a narrow binding; a double-layer binding that finishes to ¼" or ⅜" is most common. For ¼"-wide finished double-layer binding, cut enough 2⅛"-wide strips across the fabric width (about 40") to equal the quilt perimeter, plus enough additional length for seam allowances to join them into one long strip. For ⅜"-wide finished binding, cut strips 2½" wide.

Join the strips into one long piece using diagonal seams as shown on page 83. Next, fold the left end of the long strip at a 45-degree angle and press (a). Trim, leaving a ¼"-wide allowance as shown, and then fold the strip in half lengthwise with raw edges even and press (b).

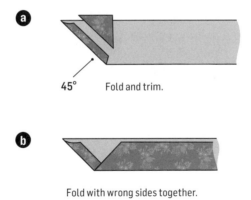

45°   Fold and trim.

Fold with wrong sides together.

ATTACHING THE BINDING

1. Engage even-feed if available on your machine, or attach a walking foot.

2. If you haven't done so already, machine-baste the quilt layers together a scant ¼" from the quilt top's raw edges. To prevent pulls and puckering at the corners, stitch from raw edge to raw edge instead of pivoting as you go around the edges. Stop at each edge and clip the threads. Remove the quilt layers from the machine, turn counter-clockwise, and stitch the next edge.

3. Trim the backing and batting even with the quilt-top raw edges.

4. Position the folded, pointed end of the binding at the quilt edge, 1" below the quilt-top center; pin in place, ending at the first corner. Begin stitching 1" from inner folded edge of the binding, using a ¼"-wide seam allowance and removing pins as you go.

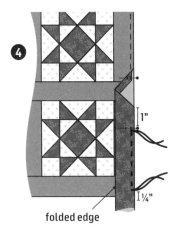

folded edge

End the stitching precisely ¼" from the raw edge at the first corner you reach. Backstitch a few stitches, clip the threads, and remove the quilt from the machine.

> *Note:* For ⅜"-wide finished binding, use 2½"-wide binding strips, sew them to the quilt with a ⅜" seam, and end the stitching precisely ⅜" from the corners.

5. Rotate the quilt 90 degrees counterclockwise. Carefully turn back the binding strip so the long edge is aligned with the next edge of the quilt in a straight line above the quilt (a). Pin the folded edge in place, and then turn the binding strip down with the new fold in the binding at the quilt raw edge. Pin in place (b).

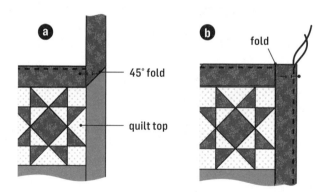

(continued on next page)

6. Continue stitching until you reach the next corner; repeat step 5 to miter the next corner. Continue in this manner until you have passed all corners and stop within 1" of where you started stitching the binding in place. *Do not remove the quilt from the machine.* Lay the end of the binding strip on top of the turned end and trim away any excess strip, leaving ¼" to tuck into the binding folded end. Complete the stitching.

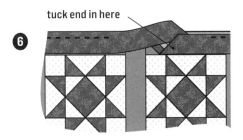

tuck end in here

7. Turn the binding toward the seam allowances and press. A mitered fold will form in each corner. Turn the binding to the backing over the raw edges and pin in place around the quilt with the folded edge just past the stitching line. Form mitered folds in the binding at each corner; pin in place.

8. Hand-stitch the binding and the mitered corner folds in place (see Hand-Stitching on the facing page).

HAND-STITCHING

Use this stitch (similar to slipstitching) to sew the binding to the quilt backing, or to add a label (page 112) to the back of the finished project.

1. Thread the needle with a single strand of all-purpose sewing thread that closely matches the binding or label color (not the backing color). Knot one end.

2. Slip the needle under the folded edge of the binding (or label), so it is hidden underneath. Sewing from right to left (reverse if left-handed), insert the needle into the folded edge, catching only a few threads of it (just a tiny "bite"). Reinsert the needle into the backing right beside the folded edge where it entered.

3. Take a short ($\frac{1}{16}$") stitch in the backing, and then catch the folded edge as before. Continue across in this manner. As you take each stitch, tug gently to snug the stitch, but not so tight that the fabric edge puckers. Stitches should be all but invisible.

4. End with several small stitches in the backing fabric.

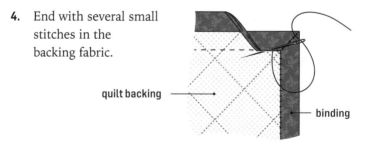

quilt backing

binding

LABELING YOUR QUILT

VINTAGE QUILTS WERE SOMETIMES SIGNED and dated by the maker, but often they were not, leaving us to wonder who was responsible for the beautiful quilts passed on to new generations. It's really a nice thing to do — to honor yourself for the work you've put into your quilts. It's also a lovely way to leave a legacy behind for those who might inherit the work of your heart and hands. While you may not think a small or utilitarian project deserves a label, it's nice to get into the habit of adding one to the back of your quilts, especially if you plan to give them away.

You can purchase simple or elaborate ready-made labels to write on, or make your own fabric labels, choosing from a variety of methods, including hand-writing on a piece of fabric, designing a label on the computer and printing on ink-jet-ready fabric, or designing and then embroidering one by hand or machine.

To make a simple label, you'll need a small piece of muslin or other plain 100% cotton fabric and permanent-ink pen with a fine tip, plus a piece of freezer paper. Ask for the pen at your local quilt shop. They may also carry freezer paper; if not, you'll find it at the grocery store.

1. Cut a 4" × 6" rectangle of muslin, or larger as needed to accommodate as much of the information commonly included on a quilt label as desired. At the least, your label should include your name and where you live,

along with the completion date, and the name of the quilter if you didn't quilt it yourself. In addition, you can include any of the following as they pertain to your work: the name of the quilt, block name(s), person for whom it was made, a pertinent quote, or coordinating artwork of your own design.

2. Machine-baste ¼" from the rectangle raw edges. Cut a matching piece of freezer paper and press its shiny side to the fabric's wrong side with a dry iron to stabilize it for writing.

3. Use a disappearing ink pen to draw writing guidelines on the fabric label. Make sure to leave some space around the label information so it's not crowded. Use a fine-point, permanent ink pen to write the information. Heat-set the ink with a dry iron; remove the freezer paper.

4. Turn under and press ¼" at the label edges, making neat corners. Pin the label in place in one of the lower corners on the quilt backing and hand-sew it in place. (See Hand-Stitching, page 111.) Remove the basting.

THE BEGINNER'S SAMPLER QUILT

Each of the blocks in the Beginner's Sampler Quilt is made of only two fabrics — a medium-light or medium print, and a dark print. Sashing strips are cut from a light print to set off the blocks. Borders and binding are cut from coordinating prints.

FINISHED SIZE

30½" square

MATERIALS*

- 2 fat quarters of light print for blocks
- 2 fat quarters of dark print for blocks and cornerstones
- ½ yard of medium-light or medium print for borders
- ½ yard of dark print for binding
- ⅜ yard of light print for sashing strips
- 1 yard of coordinating print for backing
- 34" square of thin batting

* Fat quarters (see Pre-cuts: Fat Quarters, Fat Eighths, and Others, page 16) or 44"/45"-wide quilters' cotton with 40" of usable width.

CUTTING THE PIECES

If you have not yet made the sampler blocks, refer to chapter 3 for cutting directions for each block.

Square-in-a-Square   Fourpatch   Flying Geese

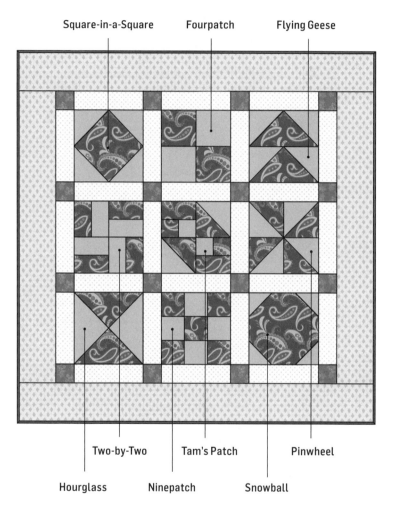

Two-by-Two   Tam's Patch   Pinwheel

Hourglass   Ninepatch   Snowball

(continued on next page)

Cut the following setting and finishing pieces:

- **Sashing Strips:** Four 2" × 40" strips; crosscut into twenty-four 2" × 6½" sashing strips.
- **Cornerstones:** One 2" × 40" strip; crosscut sixteen 2" squares.
- **Borders:** Four 3½" × 40" strips; trim to size following the directions in Step-by-Step Borders on page 81.
- **Binding:** Four 2½" × 40" strips
- **Backing:** One 34" square
- **Batting:** One 34" square

ASSEMBLING AND FINISHING THE QUILT

Note: Use ¼"-wide seam allowances throughout.

1. Make each block following the directions in chapter 3. Measure and square up the completed blocks. They should measure 6½" square before you join them into the quilt top.

2. Follow the quilt diagram on page 115 to arrange the blocks in three rows, alternating with four vertical sashing strips. Arrange the cornerstones and remaining sashing strips in four horizontal rows. Refer to Straight Sashed Setting Assembly on page 78.

3. Pin and sew the pieces together in each block and sashing row; press all seam allowances toward the sashing strips. Use chain piecing (page 50) wherever possible to speed up the sewing and pressing. Check all seams for straight stitching and accurate ¼" seam allowances. Check the points at seam edges in the blocks that have them (Flying Geese, Square-in-a-Square, Hourglass, and Tam's Patch) to make sure they weren't nipped off in the stitching. Correct stitching as needed.

4. Trim all threads. Arrange the block rows and sashing rows following the quilt diagram (page 115). Pin and sew together, following the directions in Sewing the Blocks and Rows Together (page 75). Press all seam allowances toward the sashing strips.

5. Trim the border strips to the correct size and add to the quilt top (see Cutting and Adding Borders, page 80).

6. Layer, baste, quilt, and bind your quilt following the directions in this chapter, beginning on page 84.

Congratulations! Your quilt is finished and ready to hang or to use! Now it's time to start your next quilt!

RESOURCES AND LINKS

Your local quilt shop is the very best source for your quilting needs — patterns, books, fabric, quilting tools, and other notions, as well as wonderful quiltmaking classes. If you don't have easy access to a shop where you live, there are many options for online purchases from brick-and-mortar as well as online-only quilt shops, putting the quilt resources of the country and even the world at your fingertips.

Craftsy. To locate a wide selection of PDF patterns for quilts and quilted projects, visit www.craftsy.com. Select, purchase, download, and print your favorites. Some patterns are even free. You can also register for and take online quiltmaking classes at this website, and post and share your finished projects there. You can take Craftsy classes that you've purchased at your leisure and repeat as often as necessary.

Free patterns. There are many websites that offer free patterns. To begin your search, enter "free quilt patterns" in your favorite search engine and follow the links that come up.

Techniques and problem solving. For additional quilting and sewing techniques and to find answers to common quilting and sewing questions, check out *The Quilting Answer Book* and *The Sewing Answer Book*, both by Barbara Weiland Talbert. Visit the author's webpage at www.joyofsewing.com or keep up with her doings on her blog at www.joyofsewingandquilting.com. Sign up to receive new posts on your computer.

For quilt inspiration and tutorials, join Pinterest (www.pinterest.com), the popular social-media website for web-image filing and sharing. Check out the crafts and DIY projects that abound there and save them to "virtual pinboards" that you create for personal use. It's a great site for inspiration, block and quilt designs, and patterns.

If you want to design your own quilts, you can't go wrong with Electric Quilt, software designed to help you create your own quilt designs as well as yardage charts, block-cutting directions, and cutting templates if required. A vast library of block designs are included in the program, or use the drawing tools to create your own designs. You can find Electric Quilt at many independent quilt shops, along with hands-on classes taught by experts. Or, you can order it from www.electricquilt.com.

READING LIST

To have a variety of block designs at your fingertips, consider adding one of the following excellent reference books to your quilt-book library:

Beyer, Jinny. *The Quilter's Album of Patchwork Patterns: 4050 Pieced Blocks for Quilters.* Breckling Press, 2009.

Brackman, Barbara. *Encyclopedia of Pieced Quilt Patterns.* American Quilter's Society, 1993.

As you develop your skills, you may want to invest in a few basic books on quilting. There are many available in a wide range of topics. Of all the books in my quilting library, the ones I refer to most are:

Fons, Marianne and Liz Porter. *Quilter's Complete Guide,* rev. ed. Leisure Arts, 2004.

Hanson, Joan and Mary Hickey. *The Joy of Quilting.* Patchwork Place, 1995.

For color guidance, you can't beat the following. Although these books are not new, the information is timeless. Look for both at Amazon.com or other online sources.

Barnes, Christine. *Color: The Quilter's Guide.* That Patchwork Place, 1997.

Wolfrom, Joen. *Color Play: Easy Steps to Imaginative Color in Quilts.* C&T Publishing, 2000.

INDEX

Italics indicates an illustration; **bold** indicates a table or chart.

OTHER STOREY TITLES® YOU WILL ENJOY

Fabric Surface Design by Cheryl Rezendes
Fully photographed step-by-step instructions to produce an array of surface designs using textile paints and printing ink.
320 pages. Paper. ISBN 978-1-60342-811-8.

Mend It Better by Kristin M. Roach
Creative, attractive, and easy patching, darning, and stitching, both by hand and machine.
224 pages. Hardcover with padding. ISBN 978-1-60342-564-3.

The Quilting Answer Book by Barbara Weiland Talbert
Hundreds of solutions for every quilting quandary, guiding readers through cutting, piecing, appliqué work, borders, and binding.
432 pages. Flexibind with paper spine. ISBN 978-1-60342-144-7.

Quilting with a Modern Slant by Rachel May
A glimpse into over 70 unique quilted visions, chock-full of ideas to inspire quilters of every level.
224 pages. Paper. ISBN 978-1-61212-063-8.

Sew & Stow by Betty Oppenheimer
Out with plastic bags and in with 30 practical and stylish totes of all types!
192 pages. Paper. ISBN 978-1-60342-027-3.

The Sewing Answer Book by Barbara Weiland Talbert
A friendly, reassuring resource that answers beginning and advanced sewing questions.
432 pages. Flexibind with cloth spine. ISBN 978-1-60342-543-8.

These and other books from Storey Publishing are available wherever quality books are sold or by calling 1-800-441-5700.
Visit us at *www.storey.com* or sign up for our newsletter at *www.storey.com/signup*.